Caithness

An Illustrated Architectural Guide

CAITHNESS IS THE NORTH-EAST CORNER of the Scottish mainland, beyond the Highlands. It has wide skies, rolling moors, farmland, spectacular cliffs and harbours, ringed by the mountains of Sutherland. The flow country and John o'Groats are well known, though Dunnet Head is actually the most northerly point of the mainland.

Caithness has a distinctive character due in part to a Norse influence and also to the use of Caithness stone, seen in walls, slates on roofs and flagstone fences in the fields. There are stone quarries so it is hoped that these natural materials will continue to be used.

I am delighted to write this foreword for the publication of *Caithness: An Illustrated Architectural Guide,* written by Elizabeth Beaton. I hope this book will encourage everyone to appreciate our particular heritage and that those who have not seen Caithness will visit the area.

Lyndall Leet

LYNDALL LEET
Past President
Inverness Architectural Association

© Author: Elizabeth Beaton
Series editor: Charles McKean
Series consultant: David Walker
Editorial consultant: Duncan McAra
Cover design: Dorothy Steedman, Almond Design
Index: Oula Jones

The Rutland Press
ISBN 1 873190 27 1
1st published 1996

Cover illustrations: Westerdale (Beaton)
Inserts: Left Holborn Head (Leet)
Right Carved stone head, Latheron (Leet)

Typesetting, page make-up and picture scans:
Almond Design, Edinburgh
Printed by Pillans & Wilson Greenaway, Edinburgh

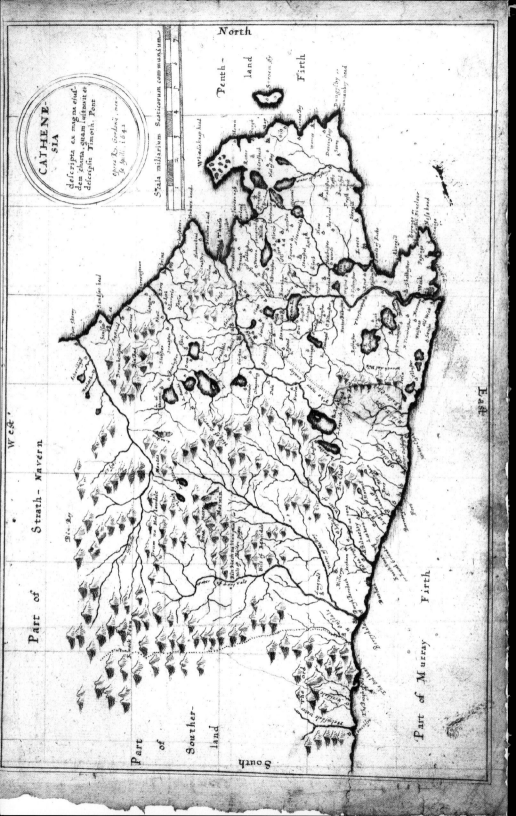

Beaton

Caithness fills the triangle of extreme north-east mainland Scotland, cut off from the rest of the country westwards by mountains and bare moorland. The steep-cliffed coastline juts out into the North Sea, from where the gales can blow with great ferocity while the Pentland Firth, between Caithness and Orkney, is legendary as a *wild and open sea*. Caithness is, in effect, insular – and, like islands, strongly individual. These *Lowlands beyond the Highlands* are different in geology, climate, settlement and building traditions from the rest of mainland Scotland. The undulating landscape stretches as far as the eye can see: vast panoramas of moors and farmland, lochs and sea, distant hills, Orkney across the Pentland Firth and – always – wide, wide skies. The built landscape of coast and country reflects this individuality; there is a varied range of buildings associated with coast and country, castle and church and the contrasting principal towns of Wick and Thurso.

An excellent corn country and a fruitful sea; the Revd Alexander Pope's description of Wick parish in 1774 is relevant to much of Caithness and reveals the twin activities that have fashioned the buildings, and much else, over the past two centuries. But the *Lowlands beyond the Highlands* have an ancient settlement history and Caithness is remarkably rich in prehistoric archaeology such as cairns, souterrains and symbol stones, too numerous and too complex to be included in this architectural guide. The associated peoples, mainly Pictish, were gradually displaced from the 9th century onwards by

Skyscape, Lythmore

Opposite *Caithness surveyed by Timothy Pont, minister of Dunnet, c.1590, and drawn by R Gordon of Rothiemay, 1642, published in Blaeu's* Atlas Novus, *Amsterdam, 1654*

Herring gutting, Dunbeath, 1920-30

Dunbeath Preservation Trust

National Library of Scotland

3

Old Keiss Castle perched at cliff edge

Dale House dovecote

Norse invaders. These later settlers brought with them their own strengths and culture – raids and war, but also trade, farming and expert nautical skills. The name Caithness is a combination of these two cultural influences: *Cait*, the Pictish province name, with the later Norse suffix *ness*, meaning promontory. Place-names of Norse origin abound, particularly with the suffix *ster* (Brabster, Sibster) originating from the Scandinavian farmstead word *Bolstadr*. Gaelic place names in the west and south identify linguistic links with neighbouring Sutherland.

Families of Anglo-Norman descent acquired land in the medieval period, including the Sinclairs (St Clair), later Earls of Caithness. It was these medieval landowners who were largely responsible for the forts and castles on coastal promontories, ringing the north and east coasts, perched on impregnable, windswept headlands. As times became more peaceful and the desire for domestic comfort stronger, these castles were either abandoned for new *lairds' houses* inland or transformed as baronial mansions; like the Castle of Mey (see p.61) these were tall but plain in the 17th and 18th centuries and baronialised in the 19th. The distinctive height of many of the 18th-century lairds' houses suggests that some plain 17th-century towers may have been remodelled in the 18th century to bring them into line with current symmetrical architectural fashion. Precise dating of such tall mansions as Freswick and Dale is therefore difficult; in-depth research and surveying is beyond the scope of this guide. Certainly sites were continuously occupied, the same names frequently repeated in Timothy Pont's map of Caithness, *c.*1590.

Dovecotes are among the earliest farm buildings; in Caithness, as elsewhere (see p.103), the oldest beehive-form dating from the late 16th century. Cotes would have been constructed only on a landowner's estate: their presence can either point to a now-disappeared mansion, as on Stroma (see p.60), or to an earlier dwelling, e.g. Westfield, Stemster (see pp.100, 106). These prestigious farm buildings also suggest that the land was productive and wealth-producing, particularly in grain, indicating an agrarian prosperity in Caithness.

Many 18th-century, symmetrical lairds' houses have distinctive wallhead *nepus* gablets and some are furnished with *scale and platt*

staircases (scale = stair, platt = flat, half landing). These are stone stairs abutting, built into and returning around, a masonry spine wall rising through the centre of the house. Some houses, such as Bilbster (see p.108) and Brabstermire (see p.61), have off-centre ridge chimneys, beside end stacks, indicating a more complex and generous arrangement of hearths. There is also a less usual M-gable, double-pile type house as at Forss (see p.94) and Westfield (see p.100).

The buildings associated with the *excellent corn country* of Caithness were large farms and small crofts, the bigger units with substantial steadings of local stone constructed by skilled masons surrounded by fields enclosed either with drystone dykes or with flagstones set up on edge. Small crofts and farms crowd marginal land, in some areas creating a remarkably populated landscape. More recently, cattle rearing has replaced grain; fields are green with grass rather than yellow with corn and tall silage towers supersede traditional barns and grain-drying kilns.

The *fruitful sea* of the late 18th century was bounteous in the 19th, largely herring. Wick, which in 1800 had no harbour worth the name, became the largest fishing station in Europe, while smaller havens and inlets, sometimes offering minimal shelter, were exploited and developed. The boom did not last, particularly in the smaller harbours, and from the 1920s herring fishing was in decline.

Top *Westfield, 18th-century, M-gable laird's house.* Above *Large grain-drying kiln, Square of Sibster*

Keiss Harbour

Church tower, Canisbay; a beacon for seamen navigating the Pentland Firth

Highland churches and manses: Thomas Telford drawings

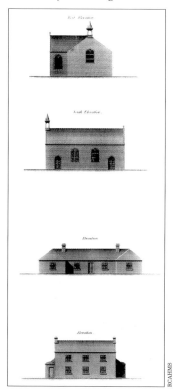

The Pentland Firth, between the north Caithness coast and Orkney, is a channel notorious for fickle tides and stormy conditions, a seaway for commercial vessels besides fishing boats. Navigation was greatly assisted in the 19th century by the construction of lighthouses: beacons for seamen and the apogee of masonry, engineering and lighting skills designed and directed by the Stevenson dynasty of civil engineers for the Commissioners of Northern Lighthouses. Caithness is ringed with examples of their expertise.

Canisbay, Dunnet and Reay, parishes bordering the Pentland Firth, have their white-harled parish churches sited on prominent coastal locations, their distinctive towers time-honoured landmarks for sailors.

The herring fishing expanded in the early 19th century, increasing the population: this in turn created new villages and crofts in the coastal hinterland (many fishermen were also crofters). These settlements were often far from the historic parish kirk, so chapels-of-ease were built in Lybster (1836), Causeymire (1842) and elsewhere. At Keiss and Berriedale (respectively Wick and Latheron parishes) advantage was taken of the 1823 Act for Building Additional Places of Worship in the Highlands and Islands of Scotland providing £50,000 for church and manse at 40 different locations. The Commission for Highland Roads & Bridges, charged with the development of the main road (A9) north, administered the project, its principal engineer Thomas Telford charged to design church and alternative manses, one single, one two storey, to cost £1500 together excluding land. Though rightly ascribed to Thomas Telford, for his was the final responsibility, credit for the design of *Parliamentary* churches must also go to his assistants William Thomson and John Mitchell (d.1824) as well as James Smith, an Inverness builder.

Peculiar to Caithness are the double-aisled, double-gabled Free Churches of *c.*1844. After the Disruption (1843) had torn the Church of Scotland (*Auld Kirk*) apart, there was a surge of church building to accommodate the new congregations and ministers who had *come out*. This Caithness type of Free Church is not found elsewhere in the Highlands. All are now disused or superseded, but still recognisable even in the guise of builder's workshop (Castletown) or farm store (Latheron). Churches built in the 1830s and 1840s are notable for their *lying-pane* (horizontal) glazing, a Scottish characteristic but in Caithness with particularly small panes of glass, as in the windows of the Wick Martyrs' Free Church, Bruan Free Church and Causeymire Mission Church, respectively 1839, 1830-40 and 1842 of which only the first named is in use.

Also distinctive, though not peculiar to Caithness, are the former United Free Churches constructed between 1905-13 after a schism with the Free Church resulted in the 1904 House of Lords ruling re-allocating church buildings. Again there was a round of ecclesiastical building, this time to a standard UF design as at Bruan and Dunbeath (both now Church of Scotland). Little wonder there is a confusing plethora of church buildings in small locations as well as the principal towns.

As in other areas of Great Britain, particularly on the coast, there was an upsurge of volunteer military activity in the mid-19th century. The 1st Caithness Rifle volunteers were established in Thurso in 1860, followed by other units in Wick and elsewhere; they were absorbed into the Territorial Army in 1908. Drill and rifle practice formed the principal training activity with drill halls in town and country as headquarters. Though adapted for other uses, a surprising number of these drill halls survive in Caithness.

The building traditions and building materials of Caithness are distinctive. The north of the district is blessed with an abundant supply of fissile flagstone, capable of quarrying as large slabs for walling, roofs and field boundaries. Their rich brown hue is pleasing, blending wonderfully with the natural landscape: the roofs sometimes attract a brilliant orange algae (colour page 50). Though these roofing slates were used on larger buildings elsewhere in Caithness, the crofts in the south were thatched because they were too far from the quarries. In Wick the local building stone is dark grey and sombre, conveniently splitting in regular horizontal sections, often of remarkable length. In Latheron to the south, the traditional homes of many farmers and crofters were long, low, narrow cruck-framed buildings, the crucks or *couples* (paired timber A-frames) supporting a heavy thatched roof. These are among the last survivals of the *longhouse* vernacular tradition in Scotland (but not peculiar to Scotland), where man and beast shared the same roof: byre,

Latheron United Free Church; standard design. The wing houses the Session Room. Photograph probably taken at opening of church, 1909

Below *Skeletal cruck framing; note herring-bone turf gable, Achlibster, Watten.* Bottom *Neat farm at Westerdale with slab fence*

7

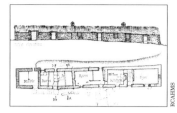

Top *Longhouse, Clashcairn*. Middle and above *Ramscraigs, Latheron*

Caithness County Council housing, designed by James Henderson

stable, barn and sometimes circular grain-drying kiln together with family living quarters. They were practical dwellings reflecting, in their time, an acceptable way of life as the homes of crofters and farmers who had attained a certain degree of prosperity. Thatch, usually over a turf base, was the usual roofing, with rushes a common thatching material. Laidhay (see p.16) is of this type, preserved as a museum.

Croft houses, both the longhouse type and more conventional three-bay cottage, are low, hugging the landscape, frequently abandoned, re-used or replaced by the ubiquitous bungalow. The large farmsteads have two-storey houses and fine steadings, the latter with arcaded cart bays with curved lintels often remarkable as examples of skilled use of local stone. Large bottle-shaped grain-drying kilns were a necessary local adjunct to these ranges.

The archaeology of the fishing industry is everywhere along the coast: kippering kilns, curing yards, harbours, fishing stores, icehouses – all distinctive though now under-used or devoted to new roles. The prosperity generated by 19th-century fishing activity is particularly evident in the expansion of Wick.

The traditional building materials of Caithness are still available, since the slates and flagstones continue to be quarried on a small scale. Their use has been pleasingly exploited in various local authority housing schemes designed by James Henderson in the early 1950s, notably his terraces with deep arched and recessed entrances derived from a similar scheme designed by Basil Spence in Dunbar, East Lothian: examples of these are found in Castletown, Lybster, Wick and elsewhere. Unusually, the architect is commemorated by one of his schemes, Henderson Square, Watten (see p.106), for he was tragically drowned. Other schemes were designed by Hugh Macdonald (Sinclair Macdonald & Son) in the 1960s and in the 1980s by Michael Lunny (Caithness District Council). There are terraces of well-designed dwellings roofed with warm brown local slates and partially clad with similar stone; flagstone garden fences often complement the schemes. Few local authorities in Scotland have such an enviable record, regrettably not always now maintained. Some enlightened clients with equally enlightened architects, continue to perceive the proven and aesthetic appeal of this ancient fabric in contemporary building design.

Organisation of the Guide

The guide follows the A9 road northward over the Ord of Caithness, Ousdale, Latheron and Wick, with a diversion to Lyth and Sibster; then to Keiss and John o'Groats. From there westward along the coast to Canisbay, Dunnet, Castletown, Bower, Thurso and Dounreay. From Reay the country is covered southwards: Shurrery, Westfield, Halkirk, Westerdale and Causeymire. Then east to Swordale and Stemster before following the A882 to Watten, from whence to Tannach to rejoin the A9 at Ulbster, completing a roughly circular route through Caithness.

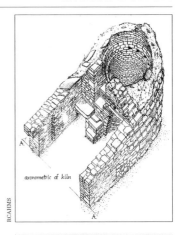

axonometric of kiln

RCAHMS

Maps

Principal locations are named on the map of Caithness: there are street maps for Wick and Thurso. The map reference numbers relate to the numbers in the text and not to pages. These maps have been prepared by Calum McKenzie.

Access

Where buildings described in this guide are open to the public, this is clearly stated at the end of the entry. When churches are locked, permission to view can usually be obtained; for this the church notice board is often helpful. Mansions, houses and shooting lodges are private, many approached by private roads: some can be seen from the public highway. Readers are asked to respect the occupiers' privacy.

Top *Axonometric drawing of croft grain-drying kiln, Achlibster, Watten.* Above *The sea is never far away: boat in centre of Wick; at rear 18th-century chimneystack*

Acknowledgements

The illustration *Steam Drifters, Wick, 1930* by P F Anson on page 27 has been donated, and the fee waived, by The Moray Council as holders of the Anson Collection. Fees have also been waived by the National Galleries of Scotland for William Daniell's prints, pp.48 & 62, and by the Scottish Record Office for the drawings on p.99. The frontispiece and illustration on colour page 72 are reproduced by permission of the Trustees of the National Library of Scotland. All illustrations credited to Historic Scotland, North of Scotland Newspapers and United Kingdom Atomic Energy Authority have been donated by those organisations.

Beaton

Drystone dyking in progress, 1994

Sponsors

Produced in association with Caithness & Sutherland Enterprise and with generous financial assistance from Caithness District Council and Caithness Tourist Board, The Manifold Trust, Braemore Estates and Property Management, Society of Northern Architects, Inverness Architectural Association and the Landmark Trust.

Beaton

Shepherd and sheep, Latheron

LATHERON

The bare hills of the Ord of Caithness separate Caithness from Sutherland, falling steeply to the sea eastwards and bounded westwards by rolling moorland. The road north hugs the coastline, following the route of medieval pilgrims who made their way to and from the great Nordic shrine of St Magnus, Kirkwall – a route further developed by Thomas Telford and the Commission for Highland Roads & Bridges between 1810-20 and later to become the A9. Latheron parish extends from the Sutherland boundary almost to Wick, a varied landscape of dramatic cliffs and headlands and small inlets contrasting with wide and endless moorland stretching away inland as far as the eye can see. This is the transition from Highland Sutherland (*southlands*) to the *Lowlands of the North*. The coastal strip has the better agricultural land with farms and thickly scattered crofts, interspersed with the occasional laird's house, while coastal villages were originally devoted to fishing. Inland crofting, combining some sheep husbandry, provided a hard-won livelihood, for the land was poorer and more exposed. Many of the menfolk combined crofting with the sea, leaving home to fish during the season as exemplified by Tormad in Neil Gunn's epic *The Silver Darlings* (1941).

Ousdale broch

Brochs are circular stone buildings with characteristic double-skinned drystone masonry walls, thought to have been constructed between 100BC and AD100 as defensive farmsteads. They were usually approximately 40ft (13m) high with battered external walls without openings except for the low entrance tunnel, flanked by a small mural guard chamber. The principal concentration is in the Highlands, Western and Northern Isles, though a few have been identified in central and southern Scotland.

OUSDALE AND BADBEA

There has long been settlement in the wide green bowl of **Ousdale**, including the vanished early 18th-century *House of Ausdale*: the archaeology of this centuries-old settlement pattern is evident today. The old track along the coast has seen much upgrading since first traversed by medieval pilgrims to become a section of the A9.

Ousdale broch, *c*.100BC-AD100

One of the best of its kind in Caithness, with

walls standing approximately 6ft (2.74m) high
and the entrance passage unusually furnished
with two sets of door checks. It is sited on a
defensive shoulder projecting into the valley
where the Ousdale Burn flows into the sea.

Former **run rig** (ridge and furrow cultivation
strips) can be seen from the road when the sun
is low, evidence of past agriculture and
settlement, the crude turf huts of the *cottars*
long gone. The pattern of large, drystone-dyked
fields reflects the farming improvements of
*c.*1800.

Ousdale Farmhouse, dated 1804
Plain, regularly fronted, two-storey, improved
farmhouse, built by James Anderson whose
other interests included the fishing harbour at
Rispond, NW Sutherland (see *Sutherland* in
this series). In its time, the farm has served as
Home Farm to the Duke of Portland's estate at
Berriedale (see p.12). There is a thriving
modern tweed **mill** and millshop: *open all year
round*

Ousdale Bridge, *c.*1815, Thomas Telford
A tall, narrow, single-arched, heavily buttressed
bridge spanning the Ousdale Burn gorge, now
bypassed. By the roadside there is also a
diminutive former mid-19th-century **school**,
too small to be readily recognised as such.

Top *Entrance, Ousdale broch.*
Middle *Ousdale Farmhouse and
tweed mill.* Above *Old school*

Badbea, early 19th century
Deserted settlement clinging to bare moorland
and cliff edge established to accommodate
families evicted from Langwell most of whom
subsequently emigrated to New Zealand. Tall
obelisk **memorial**, 1912, dedicated to residents
of the village, particularly John Sutherland
(1788-1864) who emerged as one of *the men*, a
leader endowed with *personality and gifts*.
Footpath signed from A9; lay-by car park

*Memorial and remains of settlement,
Badbea*

BERRIEDALE

Sited in a deep wooded cleft at the meeting place of the Berriedale and Langwell Waters, Berriedale village is approached either from north or south up and down steep hills with alarming gradients. The village is a sheltered oasis inviting the traveller to linger awhile to enjoy the wooded valley and to visit the shore via a meandering village street and swaying footbridge.

Langwell House, 18th-century core with crowstepped gables, the many subsequent additions creating a rambling white house crowning the hill above Berriedale village. The most recent addition to the Langwell skyline is a three-vaned **wind generator** erected in the 1980s to produce electricity. Fine **walled garden** sited one-and-a-half miles up Glen Langwell. *Signed from A9, open to public June-September*

War Memorial, 1919, Sir Ernest George and Alfred Yates
Dignified pedimented plinth surmounted by statue of St Andrew. Paired early 19th-century single-arched **bridges** (bypassed) span the Berriedale and Langwell Waters close to where they join before flowing to the sea. **Welbeck Estate Office**, early 19th-century, white-painted, regularly fronted house; nearby house with antler-decorated gable forms part of an old **smithy**.

Berriedale is a manicured village associated with Langwell House and the Duke of Portland's estate; neat houses and estate workshops line the single street in a deep cleft beside the conjoined Berriedale and Langwell Waters. Former fisher **cottages** fringe the shore, the 19th-century **icehouse** associated with commercial salmon fishing (see p.15). The beach is sheltered by a rocky outcrop crowned with the ruins of medieval **Berriedale Castle**, perhaps the site of Beruvik of the *Orkneyinga Saga*. Two unusual crenellated **towers** stand as leading lights one behind the other on the hillside above the shore, their alignment an aid to seamen entering the shelter of the small estuary. These towers are known locally as *The Duke's Candlesticks* (colour page 49).

Top *Welbeck Estate Office.*
Above *War Memorial*

There are salmon fishings (in Caithness), *besides the great one on the river Thurso, in the waters of Wick, Dunbeath and Langwell; the fish of the latter* (at Berriedale) *is considered the firmest and best in Scotland.*
Imperial Gazetteer of Scotland, i, c.1858, p.219

Berriedale

Berriedale Church of Scotland and the
White House (former manse), 1826,
Thomas Telford
Both church (colour page 49) and manse of
standard Parliamentary design, both much
altered; the former with later porch and recast
interior. A plaque above the church door
records that the land was given *GRATIS* in
1826 by James Horne of Langwell. Two-storey
White House remodelled *c*.1900, gabled
addition (see p.6).

DUNBEATH
Dunbeath village lies at the mouth of the
Dunbeath Water which flows through a wide
strath and out to sea close to the harbour on
the north side at Portormin. The wide bay is
flanked by cliffs, crowned at the south side by
Dunbeath Castle. The population swelled in
1840 when 80 families were evicted from the
strath, many settling in the village and
subsequently employed in the herring fishing.
Seventy-six boats were fishing from Dunbeath
in 1838. Commercial salmon fishing was also
active, centred at Portormin. Balcladich is on
the south side of the river while the terrace of
houses overlooking the bay is The Village: the
latter was the birthplace and childhood home of
the celebrated writer and novelist, Neil Gunn
(1891-1973).

Whalebone Arch, probably late 19th century
Fine arch on the verge just before entry to
Dunbeath from the south. Probably made from
a whale stranded on the shore locally.

Dunbeath Castle, 14th-century origins
Perched above the ocean, Dunbeath crowns a
narrow, sea-girt headland as a dramatic, crisply
white-harled castellated mansion. Decorated
with bartizans, turrets, gunloops and merlons,

*The little Highland community
... was typical of what might be
found anywhere round the northern
and western shores of Scotland: the
river coming down out of the wooded
glen or strath into the little harbour;
the sloping croft lands, with their
small cultivated fields; the croft
houses here and there, with an odd
one on a far ridge against the sky;
the school, the post office, and the
old church, where the houses herded
loosely into a township; and inland
the moors lifting to blue mountains.
On flat ground by the harbour were
the cottages of most of the regular
fishermen, but many of the crofters
also took part in the fishing seasons
... Sea fishing and crofting were the
only two occupations of the people ...*
Neil Gunn, *Highland River, 1937*.
Neil Gunn was a native of
Dunbeath, to which he referred as
Dunster in the excerpt quoted above.

*Left Dunbeath Castle, c.1875,
George Washington Wilson
Collection. Below Whalebone Arch.
Bottom Dunbeath Castle*

Former laundry, Dunbeath Castle

*In 1452, **Sir George Crichton**, Lord High Admiral of Scotland ... heired Dunbeath from his mother, and was created Earl of Caithness, a Sinclair title, by the young James the Second. He held neither Dunbeath nor the earldom long, for the Crichtons fell almost as quickly as they rose. By 1507 Dunbeath was in Innes hands, but from them passed to Alexander Sinclair, son of William, 2nd Sinclair Earl of Caithness, and Elizabeth Innes his wife, in 1529. In 1624, John Sinclair of Geanies, second son of Sinclair of Mey, who had made a fortune as a merchant, bought the property, and by him the present work was mainly erected.*
Nigel Tranter, *The Fortified House in Scotland*, v, 1970, p.89

Portormin Harbour

it is one of the most spectacular Highland castles. The earliest-known record is 1387, though such an impregnable site was probably exploited before that. Substantially, however, the present building originates from *c.*1624, erected by John Sinclair of Geanies (see *Ross & Cromarty* in this series). Sinclair's castellated mansion (fronting earlier work including tower) was oblong, with a main north entrance front with advanced stair towers and two-storey angle bartizans. In the mid-19th century there were rear alterations and additions, including a wing with three-light oriel window and a porched entrance, both overlooking the sea. The building we see now is the version remodelled by John Bryce in 1881. He inserted more windows in the main front, their size and distribution sympathetic with the earlier fabric; elsewhere he enlarged and altered the fenestration to lighten the interior and take advantage of the coastal view. The tower acquired baronial character with a crenellated wallhead. He redressed the round-headed main doorway, framing it with a cable hoodmould with knotted terminals similar to those created earlier by his architect uncle, David Bryce, for Ackergill (see p.47) and Keiss (see p.55).

The late 19th-century baronial **stable** complex is also in the style of John Bryce. There are walled gardens and an interesting Edwardian single-storey **laundry** screened from the castle with a walled enclosure. This has a symmetrical frontage lit by paired round-headed windows. Opposite the gate lodge an 18th-century lectern **dovecote** stands in a *wild garden* (see p.103).

Dunbeath Bridge, 1989, Sir Alexander Gibb & Partners
Dramatic flyover superseding the single-arch Telford **bridge**, 1809-15, both spanning the Dunbeath Water. Early 19th-century corn **mill** at Inver, by the old bridge; *picnic site and heritage trail*

Dunbeath Heritage Centre
Former late 19th-century village school overlooking the bay, the gabled stone building fronted by a walled playground. The centre has displays of local interest including natural history, local history, photographic collection. *Open during the summer months.* **Dunbeath Ross Church of Scotland** (former United

Free), 1907; standard L-plan UF church with entrance gable lit by multi-light window, apex bellcote above; session room in wing.

Portormin Harbour, 1892 incorporating earlier work, James Fraser, civil engineer Early 19th-century, three-storey, five-bay **fishing store/warehouse** with gable forestairs leading to upper storey; symmetrical frontage with shuttered windows. **Icehouse** and salmon fishers' **bothy**, both early 19th century. The vaulted icehouse is built into cliffside, the projecting gable turf-thatched to improve insulation, and furnished with a chute through which ice was emptied into the inner chamber; the outer room is for fish preparation and packing. The bothy is a single-storey crowstepped cottage for use of salmon fishers undertaking seasonal work. Two rooms fitted with bunks for four fishermen and a smaller office/bunkroom for foreman.

Top Salmon fishers' bothy, Dunbeath. Above Salmon fishermen, Dunbeath c.1920

The Village

An attractive terrace of mid-19th-century gabled and dormered cottages overlooking the bay, fronted by steeply sloping gardens.

BRAEMORE

Reached from Dunbeath by a winding road over the moors, Braemore (Gaelic: large brae) is a scattered settlement where the valley of the Berriedale Water widens, enclosed by hills and dominated by the jagged, tooth-like Maiden Pap. A *secrett and remote place*, once with two pre-Reformation *chapells*, that north of the Langwell Water at Braenaheglish (the brae of the church), perpetuated in the hill known as *Braigh na h-Eaglaise*. The other *chapell* was about *20 paces west of the House of Braemore … residence of George Gun of Braemore*, probably on the site of the present Braemore Lodge. Here, *c.*1726, *The greatest part of the image of the Sanct* (sic) *worshipped in the Chapell of Braemore stands yet in timber there*.

Braemore Lodge, mid-19th century Deep-eaved and homely, the low reddish rubble shooting lodge has tall chimneystacks and piended roof; piended dormers break eaves and the centre entrance is flanked by late 19th-century canted bay windows. Fine single-span, arched rubble **bridge** dated 1841 spans the Berriedale Water.

Salmon were an historic source of wealth, either netted or trapped by osier river traps or *cruives*. Until *c.*1800 the fish were salted and exported in barrels: afterwards parboiled in pickle. The boiling houses, with large hearths, and the icehouses are a feature of salmon stations. Ice was collected from rivers or specially constructed shallow ponds and stored in semi-subterranean stone vaults; if compressed and drained, it would keep up to a year. Packed in ice, the fish were exported by sea to urban markets.

Braemore Lodge, c.1930

Historic Scotland

Laidhay

LAIDHAY

1 **Laidhay**, early 19th century
Traditional long single-storey vernacular
farmhouse peculiar to Caithness, particularly
to Latheron, a derivation of the cruck-framed
(traditional type of modern A-frame) *longhouse*
sheltering both man and his stock in a single
linear structure, by no means considered a poor
or mean dwelling. The whitewashed rubble,
thatched building originally contained, under
one roof, stables, dwelling and byre. The
domestic living spaces are subdivided by box
beds. Separate small **barn** features long
elevations with opposing winnowing doors to
exploit prevailing winds, the thatched roof
supported by tortuously intertwined wooden
cruck trusses, the jointing necessitated by the
shortage of good timber in the area. Laidhay is
now a Caithness crofting museum. Sited on the
A9 just north of Dunbeath. *Open during the
summer months*

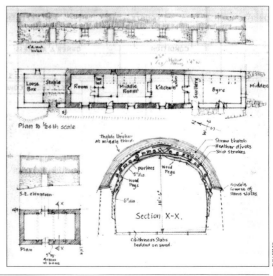

RCAHMS

*Plans and elevations, farmhouse
and barn, Laidhay*

LATHERONWHEEL

Latheronwheel (Janetstown), linear village established 1835 by Captain Robert Dunbar, the landowner whose wish that it be known as Janetstown, after his mother, was largely ignored. Houses line the single street, curving down to the small harbour snuggling between rocky outcrops, first constructed in early 19th century but altered by D & T Stevenson, 1851-2. Incredibly, for its size, this was haven to 50 vessels at the peak of the herring fishing. Single-span, hump-back **bridge**, *c.*1726, carried an earlier coastal road over Burn of Latheronwheel, often wrongly credited to General Wade. **Latheronwheel Hotel** dated 1835 and 1853, the latter probably recording alterations to this first building in the village. **Melbourne House**, plain mid-19th-century street frontage, with the surprise at the rear of prominent paired bowed bays.

*The **VILLAGE OF JANETSTOWN** which has been named as a mark of respect after LADY DUFELS (sic, correct spelling, Duffus) the mother of the proprietor the HONBle CAPTAIN ROBERT DUNBAR. This is the first house built in the village by the present occupier COLIN DUNBAR 1835.*
Inscribed datestone, Latheronwheel Hotel

Top *Latheronwheel Bridge.* Above *Melbourne House.* Left *Latheronwheel House*

Latheronwheel House, early 18th century Originally a simple two-storey dwelling house, enlarged and somewhat overwhelmed in Scots Jacobean style in 1851-3 by David Bryce.

The House of Latheronwheel presently possessed by Patrick Dunbar of Bowermadden, who has erected this year a stone bridge of a large arch which will be of great use not only to the whole Parish but to all that travel that road.
Extract from description of Latheron parish in 1726, MacFarlane's *Geographical Collections*, i

LATHERON

Small settlement at junction of A897 to Thurso and ecclesiastical centre of large, sprawling parish (colour page 72).

Gillivoan

Gillivoan, late 18th century
A typical Caithness laird's house with a symmetrical three-window frontage and centre wallhead gablet. The house is said to have been used as a Free Church manse after the Disruption of 1843 until the neighbouring (old) **manse** was constructed in 1865. Disused *c.*1844 **Free Church** of the double-gabled type

peculiar to Caithness (see pp.6 & 7). Inserted in the drystone dyke opposite are strange carved stone heads with elongated features.

Latheron Church of Scotland (former United Free), 1909
Simple building of standard UF L-plan with session room in wing; gabled front lit by large window and surmounted by a bellcote: plain clasped angle pilasters are an additional decoration.

Old Latheron Parish Church (Clan Gunn Heritage Centre), 1725-38, north aisle and domed bellcote, 1821-2, William Davidson, on earlier site
T-plan church stands within a closely packed burial ground overlooking the sea. Plain north gable frontage enhanced by square bellcote with round-headed openings in each face topped by small faceted dome. Small burial enclosure of the Sinclairs of Dunbeath, incorporating the head of a medieval lancet window built against the south wall. Fine classical **mural memorial** executed, 1642, by John Diren, to Christian Mowat, wife of Sir John Sinclair of Dunbeath. Interior converted as heritage centre. *Open during summer months*

Top *Old Latheron Parish Church.*
Above *Mural memorial to Christian Mowat*

Contractors *invited to give a plan and estimate for building of an aisle (with belfry at the end of it) to the church of Latheron. Aisle to 30ft long 25ft broad within walls. To be slated with Easdale Slate and to construct a loft. Baltick (sic) wood to be made use of.*
Advertisement for tenders for church extension issued by Heritors of Church at Latheron, *Inverness Courier,* 22 March 1821

Forse House

Latheron House, simple 18th-century core
Much enlarged and aggrandised by Victorian additions.

Buldoo Bell Tower, probably 17th century
Simple, almost shaft-like belltower crowning the hilltop with wide panoramic outlook. Rubble with pyramidal apex and rectangular bell openings. From here the scattered congregation of Latheron was summoned to the church below, without a bell until 1822 (colour page 50).

FORSE
Forse Castle, probably 12th or 13th century
Perched on a craggy peninsula, originally cut off by ditch with drawbridge, now crossed by narrow causeway. Considerable remains survive of this clifftop fortress, probably abandoned in mid-17th century (colour page 49).

2 **Forse House**, 1753
Handsome white-harled, three-storey house with symmetrical five-window frontage. There are various later additions including pretty

bargeboarded dormers, early 19th-century portico and comprehensive rear extensions. Formerly Nottingham House, this was the *elegant new house* built by Captain John Sutherland of Farse (sic) *at Nottingham*, the successor to ruinous Forse Castle on the clifftop barely two miles away. At the rear, a small cottage bears an inscribed datestone recording that it was *removed from the other side of the burn and rebuilt ... in 1801.* Forse House **dovecote**, mid-18th century; fine lectern (single pitch roof), crowstepped dovecote decorated with ball finials: interior divided as two chambers, together lined with approximately 400 nesting boxes (see p.103).

Forse dovecote

Nottingham Mains, 1842
Former home farm to Forse House. Hollow square steading: inscribed plaque over gabled arched entrance reads *Erected by John Sutherland 1842.*

Mill of Forse, early 19th century
Large rubble mill with kiln at right angles; converted as dwelling and pottery, 1996, The Leet Rodgers Practice. *Pottery open to public*

The Corr, *c.*1800 onwards
Traditional small Caithness farm constructed in the Latheron vernacular (see pp.16 & 99), with long cruck-framed, thatched farmhouse incorporating byre with gable-end entry. Separate barn with later open circular mill tramp and other ancillary buildings. An interesting and rare complex which has perfectly fulfilled all the domestic and farming needs of its occupants, an outstanding example of local vernacular.

Nottingham Mains: Forse was called Nottingham well into the 19th century (Ainslie's *Map of Scotland*, 1826). The older spellings include Nottigan (1272) and Nothingane (1408); if Norse then perhaps *nauta* (cattle) and *engjar* (meadow). Other spellings are Nottinhame, Nothingham or Noddingham suggesting Nottingham in the English Midlands, perhaps the provenance of the 13th-century Canon in the Caithness ecclesiastical hierarchy who was styled *Henry of Nothingham*, possibly a relative of the medieval owners of Forse.

The Corr Left *Farmhouse (l) with byre entrance extreme right, formerly entered from scullery and kitchen barn.* Bottom left *Rear of house and barn; note rounded ridgeline indicating cruck-framed construction.* Below *Plan*

Principal entrance, Swiney House

The place name Lybster, *like so many in the settled parts of lowland Caithness, is of Norse origin … It seems likely that the mouth of the Reisgill Burn (Old Norse hris, brushwood, and gil, ravine) was an attractive area for early settlement … on a stone was found a carved cross. This stone was removed and … subsequently located beside the central parish kirk. … Further evidence of an early ecclesiastical interest in the area is provided by the old name of Lybster Bay, Halligoe, the holy geo, and the Brethren Well to the west of the burn mouth. Moreover, during the early 19th century, excavation of the land by the river to provide a harbour led to the discovery of a substantial burial ground.*
Donald Omand (ed), *The New Caithness Book*, 1989, p.120

Portland Arms Hotel, early 20th-century photograph

SWINEY
Swiney House, *c*.1730
Fine laird's house with symmetrical five-window frontage enhanced by a shaped centre wallhead gablet and keystoned and pedimented doorway. Narrow windows paired in outer bays in *c*.1730 manner. Centre, wide, rear projecting gabled stairwell. Restored 1992, The Leet Rodgers Practice (colour page 49).

LYBSTER
Lybster village flanks a long, remarkably wide single Main Street (colour page 50) above the harbour. It was begun in 1802 by the landowner, General Patrick Sinclair, though there had been some earlier settlement by the bay. He named the section of Main Street, where it joins the A9, Quatre Bras after the battle of that name in which his two sons fought in 1815. Patrick's son, Temple Frederick Sinclair, continued the expansion of the linear village; as a staunch Whig he named the four sides of the elongated central square after the politicians of the 1830s, namely Grey's Place, Jeffrey Street, Russell Street and Althorpe Street. By 1840 the population stood at 400, the number of boats in the harbour below the village rising from 14 in 1808 to 98 in 1814: by 1838 this had increased to 101, Lybster becoming the third largest herring station in Scotland after Wick and Fraserburgh.

Portland Arms Hotel, from early 19th century
Probably the inn serving travellers on the main road, newly constructed 1810-20 by the Commission for Highland Roads & Bridges: the building was subsequently altered and enlarged. Long two-storey, seven-bay range with later dormers and pedimented detailing to windows, and fronted by glazed porch of 1968. **Quatre Bras**, *c*.1815, a tall range of houses at road junction. **Main Street** is lined with regularly fronted, 19th-century houses, the symmetry of some frontages marred by modern shop windows.

Lybster Church of Scotland, 1909-10
Former United Free church in heavy Gothic; buttressed entrance gable with apex bellcote. Outside a boulder slab carved with a cross found in the Reisgill burn and initially displayed at St Mary's Church.

St Mary's Church, 1836, William Davidson
Former chapel-of-ease, now disused. Dignified
rectangular building with Gothic windows
graced by delicate intersecting glazing bars.
Constructed to serve the expanding population
too far away from the parish church at
Latheron. **Primary School**, 1934-7, Hugh
Macdonald, Sinclair Macdonald & Son. Long,
low range with generous regular fenestration
and slightly advanced gabled end bays; centre
entrance with corniced doorpiece. Some later
additions.

Mowat Place, 1953, James Henderson,
County Architect for Caithness County Council
Local authority terraced housing with deeply
recessed round-headed entrances faced with
Caithness flagstone. Henderson was
responsible for distinctive use of local materials
noticeable in similar schemes dating from the
1950s found elsewhere in Caithness (see p.8).

Harbour, from 1810
Patrick Sinclair constructed a wooden pier at
the mouth of the Reisgill Burn, below the
village and approached by a steep lane.
Thereafter, early 19th-century, symmetrically
fronted warehouse: stone quay, 1833, harbour
enlarged by Joseph Mitchell, 1850-4, again in
1883-5. At the entrance a small octagonal
harbour light, 1884. **Harbour Master's
office**, with mural barometer for the use of
fishermen. **Inver House**, late 18th-century,
two-storey building with crenellated wallhead
that was once an inn, appears on Telford's
sketch of Lybster harbour (1790).

Below *Harbour*. Bottom *Lybster
Mains*

Lybster Station, 1903
Remains only of wooden goods shed and
dwelling house serving the Wick & Lybster
Light Railway. The keen-eyed will note the old
track running parallel with the A9.

Lybster Ha' (House) or **Lybster Mains**,
from mid-18th century
Plain two-storey house, probably part of a
larger complex, on tree-girt site. This was the
home of General Patrick Sinclair of Lybster
and his son, Temple Frederick. A scroll
skewputt resembles a herring barrel, allegedly
placed there by the General to commemorate
the success of the Lybster fishing and the
source of the Sinclair prosperity!

3 CLYTH AND BRUAN

Clyth and Bruan lie between coast and moorland, largely scattered farms and small crofts. A small sheltered inlet was exploited for fishing; there is an abandoned 19th-century, three-storey curing house/fish store similar to those at Dunbeath and elsewhere on this coast.

Clyth Mains, 18th and 19th century
Substantial farm with remains of large circular grain-drying kiln against the barn gable. Also a sheltered inlet with late 18th- and early 19th-century fishing station.

Clythness Lighthouse, 1916, D A Stevenson, engineer
A short three-storey tower on the cliff edge, with circular lantern; plain lightkeepers' **cottages**.

The boundary dividing Latheron and Wick parishes runs between the two churches at Bruan. The story is told of the tinker, who with his wife and mother, regularly camped between the two buildings, proclaiming that he slept *between two parishes, two churches and two women.*

Right Bruan Church of Scotland, former UF (l) and old Bruan Free Church (r). Below *Steps, Whaligoe; over 300 steps descending cliffside to inlet*

Bruan Church of Scotland (former United Free), 1910
Plain hall church of standard UF design, the entrance gable enlivened with usual large cusped multi-light window. To rear the disused **Bruan Free Church**, former Church of Scotland mission chapel, probably 1830-40. Gaunt rectangle with long south elevation lit by tall windows still with remnants of small-paned horizontal glazing favoured by churches of this period in Caithness (see p.7). The SPCK missioner at Bruan *came out* in favour of the Free Church in 1843 which eventually took over the building.

WHALIGOE

Whaligoe (whale *geo* or inlet of whales) is a narrow cleft enclosed by steep cliffs between two headlands; allegedly 365 (one for each day of the year) stone **steps**, some probably dating from mid-17th century, snake their way down to the **landing place**, with occasional (essential!) resting places. The platform-style landing stage is perched on a ledge above the sea, the boats winched up and lashed down in poor weather. On the cliff above the geo stands an early 19th-century, regularly fronted herring station with manager's house with rear-walled **curing yard**. In 1640 *Quhalgw* (sic) *with the fishing of the port and the corfhous* (salmon-curing house) *of the same* was associated with salmon fishing.

ULBSTER

An area of scattered crofts, some of them with traditional features such as thatched barns and single-storey cottages. On the west side of the A9 at Ulbster is an impeccably thatched traditional **cottage** and **byre**, the handiwork of a local thatcher, Mr Sinclair who died in 1995.

Mains of Ulbster, late 18th century Plain two-storey farmhouse with wide three-bay frontage, later porch, narrow windows and graded local slate roof. In the kitchen a 17th-century chimney mantel carved with the Sinclair coat of arms, re-used from a former tower house or mansion. This was presumably somewhere close by, overlooking the wide valley descending to the sea.

Ulbster burial ground, site of medieval St Martin's chapel. The centrepiece is the **Sinclair mausoleum**, 1700, restored 1995, The Leet Rodgers Practice. Square harled rubble, with first-floor entrance reached by a wide flight of nine stone steps. The elegant ogee roof is of complex carpentry, cunningly laid with heavy local slates, yellowed with algae and topped with fretted iron pennant dated 1700 with the worn letters IMS, possibly Master John Sinclair.

... there is a haven for fishing boats, called Whaligo, which is a creek betwixt two high rocks. Though the height of one of these rocks is surprizing, yet the country people have made steps by which they go up and down, carrying heavy burdens on their back; which a stranger, without seeing, would scarcely believe. This is a fine fishing coast.
The Revd Alexander Pope's description of Whaligoe in Thomas Pennant, *A Tour of Scotland in 1769*, 3rd edn, 1774

The broad sheltered valley was the ancestral home of the Sinclairs of Ulbster (later of Thurso Castle), whose most famous son was **Sir John Sinclair of Ulbster**, 1754-1835, *Good Sir John*, Member of Parliament for Caithness. He was the first President of the Board of Agriculture established by William Pitt, serving 1793-8 and 1806-13. A great collector of information, he cajoled, harried and persuaded the parish ministers and others to write detailed parish descriptions in the 1790s. The resulting 21 volumes of *The Statistical Account of Scotland* constitute a unique detailed record of population, agriculture, industry, buildings and much else in Scotland. He contributed the section on Caithness in *The Report on the Agriculture of the Northern Counties*, a series of agricultural surveys which he also instigated, published over 25 years from the 1790s. *The most indefatigable man in Britain.*
R Mitchison, *Agricultural Sir John, The Life of Sir John Sinclair of Ulbster, 1754-1835*, 1962

Sinclair mausoleum, Ulbster burial ground and Mains of Ulbster

Sinclair mausoleum, Ulbster

A worn inscription is transcribed as:
Thou who desires ane humbling
Sight to see come in behold
What thou ere long must be.
The stone-flagged upper chamber is fitted with a small hearth, presumably to warm chilly mourners: below this a rubble barrel-vaulted burial chamber reached through a trap door. The vault is D-ended with a narrow shelf or scarcement about 2ft (0.62m) from the floor, too narrow to serve as coffin rest and perhaps structural.

Square, drystone-walled **graveyard**, the entrance flanked with handsome rusticated ashlar gatepiers topped with attenuated urn finials. These piers must also date from 1700 and are in sophisticated contrast to the rubble walling.

SARCLET
Sarclet, *c*.1800
Clifftop linear crofting settlement; below the deep sheltered inlet was once a boat haven with *c*.1800 two-storey fish-curing house and remains of a windlass to pull the boats up the shelving beach. Telford noted the haven in 1790; soon after this the clifftop village and haven were developed by David Brodie of Hopeville, a tenant of Sir John Sinclair of Ulbster, who unsuccessfully attempted to name the settlement Brodiestown. The single street survives, though the flanking cottages are no longer thatched.

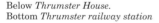

Sarclet

THRUMSTER and RAGGRA
Thrumster House, *c*.1800 and later
Simple two-storey, three-window symmetrical house forms central and original core, the plain fenestration later enlivened with hoodmoulds and the frontage lengthened with low, slightly set-back wings. The house was doubled in depth, *c*.1840, with an unusual rear staircase wing lit by a large Gothic window with intersecting glazing bars.

Below *Thrumster House.*
Bottom *Thrumster railway station*

Thrumster railway station, 1903
Small wooden station building beside track of former Wick & Lybster Light Railway. Simple but dignified rectangular building with vertically boarded walls, brick chimneystack and piended slate roof. The rear of the building faces the road, hiding the canopied frontage, long, multi-pane windows and centre door. Traces of the line can be noted along the A9.

Thrumster Church of Scotland, 1893
Expressive rectangular rubble church lit by
small round-headed windows; angle buttresses
rise above wallhead as plain finials, one
housing a flue and chimney-can. Stained-glass
chancel window, 1897, and bell, 1995 – the
latter gifted by Lady Jessamine Harmsworth in
memory of members of her family.

Thrumster Church of Scotland

Raggra
Scattered crofting settlement between the A9
road and Loch of Yarrows. The longhouse
tradition survives, though most are ruinous or
incorporated as outbuildings, while the owners
live in new bungalows. **Burnside**, early 19th
century and now ruinous, shared a single entry
for man and beast. The longhouse at **Roadside
Croft** (bungalow named Duneiston) dates from
1847, with separate entries for dwelling house
and byre: the parallel barn added in 1897. The
latter was newly rush-thatched over an
original turf base by the fourth-generation
owner in 1995 (colour page 50).

4 **Hempriggs House**, dated 1692 and 1875
White-harled and plain, two-storey house of
various builds. The rambling house is of 19th-
century appearance, but the core is earlier
and the site even earlier. The frontage,
probably 1692, with small windows faced
with long and short dressings (see also
Holbornhead, p.93), has a large centre canted
two-storey porch dated 1875. A re-used 17th-
century lintel over a blocked garden door is
inscribed CERI MANI MEMENTO MANE (*Of a
morning remember the Creator's hand*).
Hempriggs was until recently the property of
the Duff-Dunbars of Hempriggs and Ackergill
(see p.47), who played an eminent role in
Caithness history. The family, both Dunbar
and Duffs, originated from Moray and
Banffshire: Hempriggs Castle stood on a farm
of that name west of Forres (Moray).
Hempriggs House is now a residential home
(colour page 50).

Castle of Old Wick

Castle of Old Wick, 12th or 13th century
Ruinous, rectangular rubble tower
dramatically sited on a narrow headland. The
castle was originally separated from the
mainland by a ditch spanned by a drawbridge.
Grassy mounds indicate former outbuildings
clinging precariously above vertical cliff.
Guardianship Monument; open at all times

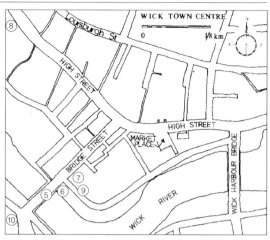

WICK

Wick is an ancient town, a royal burgh from 1589, which grew up on the north bank of the Wick River where it flows into Wick Bay. The name Wick or *Vic* is Old Norse for bay. The early small burgh developed along the north side of the tidal Wick River, initially crossed by boat. The sinuous old **High Street** follows the line of the river joined at right angles by later **Bridge Street**, both streets bustling during the day. There is a web of small lanes, a reminder of the many changes of direction caused by the siting of new bridges and establishment of Bridge Street as a principal highway.

The earliest bridge, wooden and by 1812 *much decayed*, spanned the river near today's Presto supermarket, upstream of the Bridge of Wick. Thomas Telford bridged the river in 1805 further downstream, between the Bridge of Wick and the modern concrete bridge; this was

Below Plan of Wick, c.1805 (published in 1812). Right *Aerial view, Wick Harbour, 1991*

closer to the harbour with its burgeoning
fishing industry and linked the old town on the
north bank with the new centre of
Pulteneytown. Telford's bridge has gone. The
principal bridge from 1877 was, and still is, the
Bridge of Wick linking the main thoroughfare
of Bridge Street with the A9.

Top *Wick Harbour, 1989.* Above
*Bridge Street, the commercial and
civic heart of Wick*

Until the early 1800s Wick was little used as
a port, for Staxigoe to the north provided better
shelter for shipping while Thurso was the more
important commercial entrepôt. The need for a
harbour was bemoaned by the minister in 1793
and finally begun *c*.1805, together with
Pulteneytown south of the river: both harbour
and new town were planned by Thomas Telford
for the British Fisheries Society. Wick grew fast

*Steam drifters, 1930: monochrome
painting by P F Anson executed in
1972*

throughout the 19th century as an important
centre, becoming the largest herring fishing
port in Europe. Harbourage was extended
continually while urban expansion brought with
it a need for larger and more imposing public
buildings: the vibrant commerce required
banks, concentrated in Bridge Street and High
Street. Associated fishing concerns such as net
making, roperies and cooperages clustered
around the harbour while housing expanded for
both fisherfolk and merchants: plain housing
for the fisherfolk, elegant terraces and villas for
the merchants. To help satisfy the need for
improved transport, the Highland Railway
reached the town from Inverness in 1874.

The local building stone (mostly from near Hempriggs) is sombre grey, splitting into long narrow sections. It is not unusual to find single sections measuring 12ft-13ft (3.66m-3.94m) as monolith door and window lintels or sills. Some 19th-century prestigious public buildings have imported sandstone cladding which lent itself to moulding or rustication. In contrast the *mono-harling* of most late 20th-century development creates a bland built landscape.

Fishing declined in the 20th century; some other activities have developed, notably the Caithness Glass factory established on the outskirts of the town in the 1960s. Wick is the administrative centre for Caithness local government now within The Highland Council.

This bridge, opened in July 1877, was crossed when in course of construction on 1st Oct 1876 by Their Royal Highnesses the Prince and Princess of Wales, Prince John of Gluckenburg, The Duke and Duchess of Sutherland and a distinguished party on the occasion of a visit of their Royal Highnesses to Wick.
Inscribed plaque on Bridge of Wick

Below *Royal Bank of Scotland.*
Right *Bridge of Wick and Wick River*

Wick Town Centre, north of the Wick River

5 **Bridge of Wick**, 1875-7, Murdoch Paterson, engineer
A wide three-arched bridge with triangular cutwaters rising as parapet refuges. From the Bridge of Wick, Bridge Street appears an urban defile flanked at right by the Royal Bank of Scotland and left by the massive, triple-gabled riverside elevation of the former Station Hotel.

David Rhind, 1808-83, trained in London with Augustus W N Pugin, before setting up practice in Edinburgh. He was only in his early twenties when he designed the Commercial Bank, Wick (the design was also used in Falkirk), subsequently becoming architect to the Commercial Bank. These banks reflect the elegance of Edinburgh classical taste; Rhind's French and Gothic essays are more ponderous. His elegant bank and heavy courthouse in Bridge Street, make interesting comparison.

Bridge Street
6 **Royal Bank of Scotland** (former Commercial Bank), *c.*1829-30, David Rhind
A magnificent building of much architectural beauty. Restrained classicism from Edinburgh, the first floor graced with Ionic-columned screen above advanced ground-floor centre entrance. Street and river frontage faced with polished sandstone ashlar, the principal windows corniced within moulded jambs. Balustraded single-storey terraced wing projects to overlook the river; later first-floor canted bay window.

7 **Town Hall & Tolbooth**, 1825-8,
Robert Reid
Stalwart civic classicism with a flavour of the
traditional early 18th-century Scottish burgh
tolbooth replacing its predecessor in Tolbooth
Lane. Regular-fronted building generously lit
with long windows. Imposing centre advanced
square tower incorporated in arcaded loggia
fronting the street and rising as octagonal clock
tower crowned by a tall cupola. Dignified, first-
floor council chamber with deep plaster frieze,
reached by wide balustraded staircase.
Tolbooth with cells originally filled rear wings.

Robert Reid, 1774-1856,
*Edinburgh, was the principal
government architect in Scotland
during the first half of the
nineteenth century ... His long career
as a public architect began in 1803
when he was commissioned to design
the new Law Courts in Parliament
Square, Edinburgh. In 1808, on the
strength of this important public
work, he obtained a warrant
authorising him to use the title
'King's Architect and Surveyor in
Scotland'. This was purely honorary.*
Howard Colvin, *A Biographical
Dictionary of British Architects
1600-1840*, 3rd edn, 1995

Sheriff Court (l) and Town Hall (r)

Sheriff Court, 1862-6, David Rhind
Italianate but with Frenchified, slated centre
gable rising as tower crowned with elaborate
cast-iron cresting. Cast-iron, barley-sugar twist
balustrade to main staircase.

17-21 Bridge Street, late 19th century
Three-storey frontage with shops in ground
floor; above this the viewer can appreciate the
full impact of contrasting pale sandstone and
dark Wick rubble walling crowned with an
unusual two-tier wallhead cornice.

The west side of Bridge Street begins with the
Riverside Nursing Home, dated 1866 (former
Station Hotel); substantial three-storey building
overlooking Bridge Street with dominant three-
gabled side elevation flanking the river. The
very large paving stones in front of the entrance

are a reminder of the once-thriving Caithness flagstone industry centred on Castletown and Thurso: pretty art nouveau cast-iron railings are half hidden with boarding.

Bridge Street Church of Scotland (former Free Church), 1862-4, William J Gray
Gothic; sandstone street frontage dominated by large traceried window with a soaring spire rising from a barely advanced square tower with porch in base, a landmark visible from most of the town. Lofty galleried interior; imposing pulpit below bracketed canopy.

Bank of Scotland (former British Linen Bank), reconstructed 1933-5, John Keppie & Henderson
Striking monumental frontage in 1930s modern Scots style. Polished dark granite ground floor with sandstone ashlar above. Carved stone armorial by Scott Sutherland: carved finials above depressed ogee window lintels in second floor depicting stylised leek, thistle and rose. In contrast the **Clydesdale Bank** (former Town & County Bank), 1875, Russell Mackenzie, sports a Venetian

Above *Bank of Scotland, Bridge Street, 1933-5 frontage.* Right *Clydesdale Bank*

Renaissance palazzo frontage richly decorated with sculpted heads and roundels; elegant door furniture to main entrance.

Old Parish Church

High Street

8 **Old Parish Church**, 1820-30, John Henry
Imposing rectangle with chunky Gothic detailing, its finely tooled dark local stone bulk enlivened by contrasting pale sandstone dressings accentuating the regular, elegant, Tudor arched doors and windows, all of the latter with their original multi-pane glazing. Orange algae, common in Caithness, colours the south pitch of the roof creating an unexpected splash of colour amidst the enclosing trees. Gabled entrance front with tall windows and square tower crowned with crenellated wallhead, angle pinnacles and squat gableted spire. The wide roof span is carried internally without supporting columns. Extensively remodelled internally, 1993-4, D A Renwick Associates. The church area is accommodated at first-floor level incorporating former gallery while the ground floor has been adapted for other parish activities.

The church occupies an earlier site, its predecessor described in 1793 as a *very old, a long dark, and ill-constructed building*. The

Left Sinclair of Stirkoke aisle, Old Parish Church. Below Detail, Sinclair of Stirkoke aisle

31

Top *Dunbar of Hempriggs enclosure.* Above *Father Time with hour-glass and scythe, Dunbar of Hempriggs memorial*

The Dunbar of Hempriggs memorial reveals vigorous early 18th-century funereal imagery, the emblems of mortality and immortality. Winged Father Time with his scythe, hour-glass, coffin, bones, *Deid Bell* (rung at funerals) and sexton's tools all represent the inevitability of death. Of emblems of immortality there are *winged souls,* cherubic faces with wings whose role it was to carry the departed to Heaven where their arrival was trumpeted by *angels of the resurrection*, portrayed as contemporary gentlemen wearing wigs.

Right *Dunbar of Hempriggs memorial.* Below *Kirkhill*

roofless, buttressed **Sinclair aisle** of the *very old* church was *repaired and ornamented agreable to the will of the late Miss Sinclair of Stirkoke* in 1835 with crenellations and fluted urn finials, the style reminiscent of William Robertson, Elgin (see also RC Chapel, p.39).

A second, 19th-century, tall, roofless bullfaced (stylised rustic) masonry enclosure re-houses the magnificent, classical, early 18th-century pilastered **mural memorial** to the Dunbars of Hempriggs and Ackergill, probably removed from the earlier kirk. The arms of Sir William Dunbar (died 1711) and his wife Margaret Sinclair are framed by the segmental broken pediment flanked by flat-chested cherubs in wigs blowing trumpets; there is (damaged) undercut ribbon moulding, while a full range of *mementi mori* decorates the panelled base complete with bearded Father Time carrying a realistic scythe, his wings intricately detailed. Undoubtedly this impressive piece of Moray sandstone sculpture originated from Elgin, where funereal sculpture flourished in the early 1700s. It has a remarkable stylistic affinity with the equally imposing mural monument to Sir Robert Gordon of Gordonstoun, 1705, Michaelkirk, Gordonstoun (see *District of Moray* in this series). Also reset in the mausoleum wall is a stone laurel wreath flanked by carved swags. **Church** and **mausolea** stand in a walled burial ground sloping down to the river and packed with upright and recumbent tombstones. **Old Manse**, 1786, stands close to the church in the High Street; two-storey, crowstepped and many subsequent alterations.

Kirkhill, 7 Church Street (corner High Street), 1830-40
Typical, unpretentious Wick townhouse; tall, two storey and attic with later canted dormers; regular fenestration and centre doorway, all enclosed by a stone garden wall.

Zig-Zag nightclub (previously Dominoes, former New Pavilion Cinema), c.1925
Art deco; cavernous entrance flanked by advanced octagons, painted magpie black and white. It was originally a roller-skating rink, thought to be the first building in Wick constructed of 6in (15cm) prefabricated blocks. In 1929 it opened as the New Pavilion Cinema, *the most commodious and luxurious place of entertainment in the North of Scotland* reported the *John o'Groat Journal*, Christmas 1929. Gutted by fire, 1996.

Zig-Zag nightclub

Woolworth's Store (former North of Scotland Bank), 1886, A Marshall Mackenzie
Modern shop front cuts into the classical Aberdeen pale grey granite frontage designed by an Aberdonian architect who favoured the building stone of his native city.

The Crescent, c.1820
Curious, dignified, three-storey, slightly concave terrace with symmetrical fenestration and blocked wallhead. Of note the curved roof made up of two demi and two complete shallow slated pyramids: a construction that must have tried the skills of both joiner and slater!

Market Place, former market area opening off the medieval thoroughfare of High Street and dominated by former **post office**, 1912, W T Oldrieve; tall, dignified Edwardian Scottish Renaissance; crowstepped with a slightly

A Marshall Mackenzie, 1848-1933, was born in Elgin, son of architect Thomas Mackenzie (d.1854 aged 39). Trained with James Matthews (his father's old partner), Aberdeen and David Bryce, Edinburgh, before travel in Europe and further study at the Ecole des Beaux Arts, Paris (perhaps the first Scot to do so). Practised in Elgin from 1870 before moving to Aberdeen in 1877 from where he retired in 1893. Amongst his most distinguished works in Aberdeen are New Kings, sympathetically neighbouring medieval Kings College Chapel, and Marischal College. The *John o'Groat Journal*, 4 April 1893, describes A Marshall Mackenzie as *very talented*. At this time his brother was Sheriff in Wick.

Former post office, Market Place

asymmetrical frontage, the rear elevation crowning the cliff-like site overlooking the river.

9 **Salvation Army Temple**, Victoria Place, 1845 Built as Evangelical Union Chapel. Austerely dignified street frontage enhanced by two long and four short first-floor (gallery) windows with multi-pane glazing. Alterations mar the original regularity of door and window openings.

George Street, Hillhead and **Louisburgh**
The northern fringes of Wick stretch out to the airport (see p.45), Caithness Glass factory and visitors' centre, and include the late 18th-century settlement of Louisburgh, laid out as a grid pattern but little housing of note; extensive local authority housing marches along Willowbank and Hillhead.

Right *Ash Villa*. Below *Detail of bargeboards and glazing*. Bottom *Caithness Glass Factory and Visitors' Centre*

Ash Villa and **Oak Villa**, George Street
Two charming *c.*1900 gabled villas of special note for their intricate and handsome wooden bargeboards, enriched with carved thistles, roses and realistic draped and swagged valences. Ash Villa is the larger, with original glazing, banded fish-scale slate conical roof to two-storey tower accommodating entrance in base and decorative cast-iron railings separating garden from road. Smaller Oak Villa has lost its original glazing. Late 19th- and early 20th-century villas and bungalows line **George Street** on the northern outskirts of the town, remarkable for the varied decorative cast-iron railings that divide front gardens from the street (colour page 52).

Caithness Glass Factory and Visitors' Centre, George Street, 1992, Wylie Shanks Long and low hugging the landscape, deeply gabled with light and airy interior, combining workplace and visitors' facilities; viewing

gallery enables visitors to observe all processes of glass-making.

Wick North Primary School (formerly North School), Ackergill Street, 1937, Hugh Macdonald of Sinclair Macdonald
Long and dignified with generous, south-facing windows and piended slate roof originally with central ridge cupola; low ashlar-faced entrance porches at each gable.

Wick North Primary School

Hillhead Farm retains a squat bottle-shape, late 18th- early 19th-century, grain-drying **kiln** at the gable end of one threshing barn, the bowed gable of another range indicating that that, too, once housed a kiln. These substantial kilns are peculiar to the larger Caithness farm (colour page 51).

Pulteneytown and south of the Wick River
Wick is approached from the south through South Road, Francis Street and Cliff Road dropping steeply down to Bridge of Wick. The area was developed in the 19th century in regular grid plan, in marked contrast with the irregular old town. Small Victorian villas and terraced housing line South Road, Francis

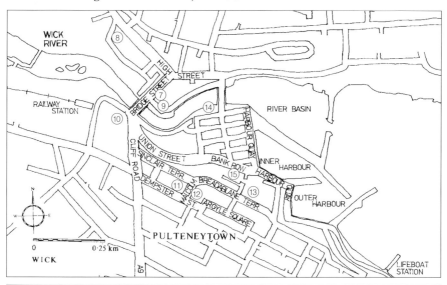

Wick High School, c.1910

North of Scotland Newspapers

Street and the residential areas about Coronation Street and West Banks Avenue. In the latter, **Wick High School**, 1909, D & J R McMillan, a compact, strong building strangely combining octagonal angle Tudor turrets with Scottish crowstepped gables. The dark masonry is generously enhanced with light sandstone dressings. Later extensions have weakened the impact of the original design.

12 Francis Street, *c.*1870
A plain villa enhanced by a profusion of fine decorative cast-iron balcony fronts, brattishing (ridge crest) and garden rails. This was originally the home of a prosperous rope merchant. In 1872 there were three parallel rope walks stretching between Macrea and Francis Streets in the area now occupied by the bowling green and Loch Street.

Alexander Ross, 1834-1925, inherited his father's Inverness architectural practice in 1853 aged 19. The first few years were slow but from 1865 until the end of the century and beyond Ross was firmly established in the Highlands. No task was too small, but where the client had the means, Ross could design complex baronial as at Skibo Castle (see *Sutherland* in this series) or rich ecclesiastical Gothic, particularly St Andrew's Episcopal Church, Fort William.

St John the Evangelist Episcopal Church, Moray Street, 1868-70, Alexander Ross

Interior, St John the Evangelist Episcopal Church

Beaton

Simple buttressed Gothic church with lancet windows and slightly lower chancel at corner of Moray Street/Francis Street. Gabled porch ornamented with squat columns decorated with stiff leaf carving. The plain interior has a braced timber roof and mainly clear window glazing, some enhanced by fine frosted engraving dated 1970 and 1994, initialled DG.

10 **Caithness General Hospital**, Cliff Road, 1983-6, Baxter, Clark & Paul
Substantial curved building of bland sandstone contrasting with dark blue/grey profiled cladding and roof, the convex front elevation exploiting the crescent-shaped site above the Wick River overlooking Bridge Street. This long north frontage dominates the town; the car parks and service bays hidden at the rear (colour page 52).

Mackay's Hotel, Union Street, 1884
Tall, filling a narrow awkward triangular plot as regally as a ship's prow, the narrow, bowed 'prow' topped by an apex chimneystack in place of a bowsprit. **Baptist Church**, also Union Street, 1868, plain street elevation lit by long, narrow pointed-headed windows linked by continuous stringcourse.

Top *Caithness General Hospital.*
Above *Mackay's Hotel*

Wick Railway Station, 1873-4,
Murdoch Paterson
Exterior resembles a dignified mart: long, low and gabled with deep-eaved roof and slated ridge ventilator. During refurbishment in 1985 by Lyndall Leet, the passenger waiting area was enhanced with Caithness flagstone floors and stone planters; the ticket office became bright and welcoming with a stripped pine interior.

Pulteneytown, from 1807
Grid layout on broad plateau above harbour and bay, the streets lined with regular, mainly two-storey, symmetrically fronted houses. With the exception of **Breadalbane Crescent**, all dwellings open on to the street; this was usual in planned towns of the era for it was thought that front gardens might be utilised as middens. The building stone is a dark schist which splits easily and can be worked in long sections. This is seen to good effect in **Breadalbane Terrace**. There is original and notable door carpentry, including both elegant panelling and robust turning, adding finesse to better quality terraces and

Pulteneytown was established by the British Fisheries Society, and laid out by Thomas Telford in 1807 on 390 acres obtained from Sir Benjamin Dunbar of Hempriggs four years earlier; the land also included sources of excellent building stone. The town was named after Telford's patron, Sir William Pulteney, former Governor of the British Fisheries Society. Like Telford he came from the Borders; born Johnstone, he changed his name after marriage to the heiress to the Earl of Bath's fortune. Argyle Square, Breadalbane Terrace, Grant Street, Smith Terrace and other streets were named after Directors of the British Fisheries Society.

enlivening the simpler houses. Fine door carpentry is a tradition in north-east fishertowns, also evident in 19th-century housing of the Moray Firth seatowns. **Sinclair**, **Breadalbane**, **Smith** and **Bexley Terraces** form a continuous series of streets fringing the high ground above the harbour, overlooking the bay. Original dwellings in **Huddart** and **Vansittart Streets** have been replaced with uninteresting local authority housing.

Sinclair Terrace

Terraced street, early 19th century at west end which is somewhat marred by shop insertions, but **No 17** is a model *c*.1830 townhouse, whitewashed plain frontage, tripartite (three-light) windows and elegant, recessed, columned and pedimented doorway with fine original panelled door. Further up the street, the terraced housing is plainer, some dwellings with original doors with wheel-motif central panel.

Top *Wheel-motif door, 10 Sinclair Terrace.* Above *Door, 17 Sinclair Terrace; handsome recessed doorpiece with fine and unusual panelled door.* Right *Wick (Carnegie) Library; classical revival elegance*

Wick (Carnegie) Library, Sinclair Terrace, 1895-8, Leadbetter & Fairley
Edwardian freestyle, occupying its corner site with grace and dignity. The angled entrance gable fronted by a semicircular portico below a Venetian window, like the long flanking ground-floor fenestration, has heavy Gibbs (blocked) detailing. To the left of the main entrance the projecting windowed stairwell floods the interior with light, in keeping with the inscription over the main door *Let there be Light*, a motto associated with Carnegie foundations. Spacious full-height entrance/stair-hall, the curved staircase leading to the long, dignified St Fergus Gallery with discreetly decorated barrel-vaulted plaster ceiling. The galleried landing accommodates a late medieval recumbent

St Fergus, patron saint of Wick

figure of St Fergus, the crisp carving the result of re-facing by John Nicolson of Nybster (see p.59), in late 19th century. The figure originated from an earlier parish church dedicated to this saint, predecessor of the present Old Parish Church (see p.56). The head is tonsured, a jewelled cross hangs around the neck, the hands are folded and the feet rest on a sleeping lion.

The church of Wick stands at the W end of the town ... It is called St Fergus Church and there is in the E end of it on the N side under a little pend, a hewn stone with a man at full length on it, which is said to be his effigie engraven on stone.
Early 18th-century description from MacFarlane's *Geographical Collections*, i, 1906, p.158

Assembly Rooms, Sinclair Terrace, from 1838
Former Pulteneytown Academy, built by the British Fisheries Society. Plain and tall with generous windows but subsequent alterations have almost obliterated the original dignity of this building enjoying a commanding position over the harbour.

11 **Wick Martyrs' Free Church** (former Secession Church), Sinclair Terrace, 1839
Plain rectangle with rusticated quoins, the local slate roof replaced with bland concrete tiles and the stone-walling coated with even blander harling. The dignified original regular fenestration with unusual small-paned horizontal glazing survives to retain some original architectural character of this church occupying corner site with Malcolm Street. The porch is later.

Peter Frederick Anson, 1889-1975, came from a naval family. He spent two years training as an architect before becoming a Benedictine monk. After leaving that vocation he devoted his life to RC ecclesiastical buildings and recording the life of fisherfolk, as a writer and artist. He left his papers and nearly 500 paintings and drawings to The Moray Council, the latter in the Anson Gallery, Buckie.

Left *Wick Martyrs' Free Church*.
Below *St Joachim's Roman Catholic Chapel, sketch by P F Anson, 1937: the coursed-rubble façade is now white harled*

RCAHMS

12 **St Joachim's Roman Catholic Chapel**, Malcolm Street, 1833-5, William Robertson
Pedimented and pilastered frontage with centre corniced entrance, the rich golden/brown sandstone dressings (brought by sea from Moray) contrasting with the later pale harl. Long, pilastered, north elevation lit by wide lunettes (semicircular windows) graced with

St Joachim's R C Chapel

St Joachim's R C Chapel. Pilastered side elevation lit by lunettes with original intersecting glazing

The Roman Catholic Chapel was constructed to serve the Catholics amongst the 7000 itinerant fishermen and female gutters who crowded into Wick (normal population in 1830s *c*.2000) during the herring season between mid-July and mid-September. The moving spirit behind its construction was Father Walter Lovi, somewhat eccentric priest of Keith, Banffshire. He collected funds in Ireland and England besides receiving local donations in recognition of his care of the sick during the cholera epidemic of 1832. Lovi frequently sailed from Buckie, on the Banffshire coast of the Moray Firth, to Wick. He obtained plans for his chapel from the Elgin architect, William Robertson, 1786-1841, who shipped Moray sandstone to Caithness for the frontage.

original intersecting glazing. Modernised interior. The frontage linked to flanking **presbytery** and **school** built in 1869.

Argyle Square
This long rectangular tree-filled square is the heart of residential Pulteneytown. Photographs of the early 1900s show the square without trees and appearing much larger. Enclosed by plain, terraced two-storey houses, it has canted angles and street entries symmetrically placed on all four sides, of which Dempster Street leads to Francis Street and the A9 while Lower Dunbar Street terminates with a steep flight of steps, **The Black Stairs**, descending to Lower Pulteneytown and the quayside. The spacious square contrasts with the harbour below, even more markedly when the harbour teemed with boats and fisherfolk.

Right *Argyle Square*.
Below *Pulteneytown Parish Church*

Pulteneytown Parish Church (formerly St Andrew's), Argyle Square, 1842
Built as a chapel-of-ease for the expanding Pulteneytown. Street entrance gable topped by chunky bellcote and lit by three large round-headed windows placed above the centre entrance, a somewhat advanced pattern for its time. Set back Old Hall at west added 1958, the New Hall to the south constructed in 1974. Galleried interior, the gallery supported by slender cast-iron, marble-ised cluster columns. Handsome original white-painted pilastered back board fills most of the south gable, almost

18th century in style, pedimented, corniced and elegantly surmounted by urns. The pulpit, pews and other furnishings are later replacements.

Wick Central Church of Scotland (disused), Dempster Street, from 1853
Gothic, the buttressed tower with faceted spire added in 1862 punctuating the Wick skyline as a landmark.

Breadalbane Crescent Left *Homes of prosperous fish merchants, unusually set back from road with front gardens.* Below *Rear paved yards flanked by fish curing and storage buildings besides accommodation for itinerant herring-gutting women.* Bottom *Nos 10-11; spacious entrances, panelled doors and large windows enhance the domestic quality of Breadalbane Crescent*

Breadalbane Terrace and **Crescent**
Breadalbane Terrace follows the high ground above the harbour, lined both sides with neat two-storey houses opening directly to the street. Former **cinema**, now social club, *c.*1925, probably Sinclair Macdonald; masonry frontage hinting at Modern Movement style. More superior is **Breadalbane Crescent**, 1860-5, eight houses in blocks of two or four dwellings set back from the street and fronted by gardens enclosed by coped walls with spearhead railings. The houses are tall, three- and five-bay dwellings, with generous windows and dormer provision unusually austere for their mid-19th-century date. Between the blocks there are entries to rear paved yards (some now gardens) with former stables, cooperages and bothy accommodation for itinerant fisherfolk including female herring gutters. These were the homes and workplaces of the herring fishing entrepreneurs.

Former Pilot Station, Smith Terrace, 1908
Presented by Sir Arthur Bignold of Lochrosque, MP: square with elegant ogee fishscale-slated roof sweeping over the wallhead to form a deep veranda supported at each corner by cast-iron columns. Sheltered benches and a commanding view over bay and harbour attract residents and visitors alike.

41

James Bremner, 1784-1856, trained in Greenock as a shipbuilder, returning to his native Caithness to establish his own business in Wick. During the next half-century he constructed over 50 vessels besides designing and building harbours. He developed remarkable expertise in raising shipwrecks, his greatest triumph being the recovery of SS *Great Britain*, the first iron-hulled vessel, which had run aground in Ireland.

Above *The Black Steps link Pulteneytown with Lower Pulteneytown and harbour.*
Right *Wick Harbour*

... on the N E coast, at present there is no place where a vessel can run into or even lye with safety ... Vessels frequenting the Herring Fishing in this quarter lye in the River of Wick but they are confined within a shallow Bar in a Narrow Channel, and so exposed to the N E that they dare not wait the equinoctial Gales, and instead of Fishing for the whole season they push off as soon as they can get anything like Cargo. They have no place but the Beach on which to land and stack their fish, and they frequently cannot get over the Bar, even to reach their Beach, but lye with their Fish in their open boats exposed to the Sun until they are spoiled. It is generally allowed that the deep sea fishing might be carried on (in) this Quarter, but no person will risk his vessel and Capital while there is no place of security for them to run into in case of Stormy weather nor any convenience whatever to enable them to carry on their business with advantage.
Report by Thomas Telford, civil engineer, May 1802

Smith Terrace and **Bexley Terrace** flank one side of the street only, overlooking Wick Bay. Very fine panelled doors survive in recessed porches of **Nos 1 & 2** Bexley Terrace (colour page 51). On the cliff edge, **memorial** to James Bremner, Wick's pioneering 19th-century harbour engineer. The grey granite obelisk is suitably adorned with cable moulding and other marine insignia.

Lower Pulteneytown and Wick Harbour

Lower Pulteneytown, linked with Pulteneytown by the steep flight of The Black Steps, fills the area around the harbour, largely occupied by herring yards and other buildings constructed during the first half of the 19th century and associated with the fishing and harbour. The first harbour included two piers and some breastwork, designed, c.1805, by Thomas Telford, for the British Fisheries Society, with George Burn as contractor for both harbour and bridge. It continued to expand throughout the 19th century, in the 1830s and 1840s under the direction of James Bremner. As fishing prospered, the quayside became lined with cooperages and herring yards, many of which are now re-used for industrial and commercial purposes. Demolition in the early 1990s for road widening, swimming pool and medical centre has altered the Lower Pulteneytown regular grid pattern of streets with Williamson Street as core.

Old Fish Market, Harbour Quay, c.1890
Probably the earliest purpose-built fish market in Scotland, retaining its original furnishings. Cheerfully painted single storey and weatherboarded with shallow piended roof fronted by deep veranda supported on slender cast-iron columns with decorative brackets (colour page 51). Fish were sold direct from the boats until the 1880s after when the introduction of cotton netting increased the catches and this

method of disposal became impractical. From then on sales were conducted from a harbourside mart. By the old mart a row of wooden fishing gear sheds provides more colour, their small scale contrasting with the wide concrete harbour piers and tall terraced housing (colour page 51).

Swimming Pool, 1993, Michael Lunny, Caithness District Council
Dark grey cladding and wide slate roof blends with the local stone. Large and low, with deep eaves and cheerful red window glazing bars.

14 **Wick Medical Centre**, 1995, D A Renwick Associates; welcoming, substantial gabled, L-plan cottagey range on riverside site. Light stone cladding with local, dark grey rustic stone facing to main entrances; perky canted oriels punctuate the attic gables.

Wick Medical Centre

15 **Wick Heritage Centre**, Bank Row, early 19th century
Complex comprising **dwelling house**, **curing yard** and a **cooperage** (colour page 50), part of terraced Bank Row abutting the cliffside with Upper Pulteneytown above. The plain street frontage has an arched pend (passage) leading to a central courtyard, notable for its fine masonry, particularly the detailing over all doors and windows. The centre (opened in 1981 by the Wick Society) records the rich fishing heritage of Caithness; it also houses the Johnston Photographic Collection of 100,000 prints and plates, the work of three generations of Wick photographers, Alexander, William and Alexander Johnston, between 1860-1950. It is an interesting and vibrant museum established by local initiative and run by local enthusiasts. *Open during summer months*

Wick Harbour, 1865; in foreground gutting crews clean herring for packing in salt in barrels for export

Above *The Round House overlooking Wick Harbour; note continuous ridge battery of chimneystacks.* Right *Lifeboat House with launching slipway*

The Round House, Harbour Quay, 1807, Thomas Telford
Sited on a bluff above the quay, two storeys with bowed outer bays linked by oversailing eaves, the shallow piended roof crowned by a long battery of chimneystacks.

Lifeboat House, 1915
Gabled and functional with chunky rubble stringcourse as sole decoration, fronted by a steep concrete slipway down which the boat would slide into the water. A lifeboat station was established at Wick in 1848, the boat-house, the earliest of its kind in Scotland, demolished for road widening in 1988. Currently the lifeboat is moored in harbour, perpetuating the long, local service *to those in peril on the sea*.

16 **BROAD HAVEN, PAPIGOE AND STAXIGOE**
Before Wick harbour was developed from 1805 both Broad Haven and Staxigoe offered shelter to trading ships and fisher boats. Staxigoe, protected from the open sea and with a shelving path to the shore, was the better of the two.

Right *Staxigoe, 1891*. Below *Haven House: Papigoe in background*

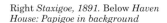

Haven House, Broad Haven, early 19th century
Traditional two-storey house perched on a rocky outcrop projecting into Broad Haven Bay. **Papigoe** strings along the road between Broad Haven and Staxigoe, a small settlement of older cottages and modern housing.

Staxigoe
Narrow sheltered inlet with 18th-century warehouses ringing the high ground above the haven. These stored incoming and outgoing goods at this former entrepôt, linked by a track to the shelving shingle beach where small boats could be pulled up when plying between the shore and shipping anchored further out in deep water. There is a short rubble pier projecting into the bay while the quay on the west side is constructed of vertically laid masonry, narrow blocks of stone placed on end.

WICK AIRPORT
An airport was established in Wick in 1933. Small, whitewashed control tower with horizontal, metal window frames; also a series of large hangars probably dating from wartime expansion, 1939-45, now used as stores.

Top Staxigoe Bay with remaining warehouses, 1994. *Above* Cliffside quay constructed of vertical masonry

SIBSTER
17 **Square of Sibster**, 18th, 19th and 20th centuries
Farm steading notable for wide range of buildings mirroring agricultural development and change through three centuries. Eighteenth-century **kiln-barn** with opposing winnowing doors at each end of the winnowing passage and terminating with a circular kiln at the north gable. The **kiln** (see p.5), which has massive walls and a conical roof with apex vent, is constructed of slivers of rubble shale. The threshing floor and hand flail were superseded in early 19th century by machinery motivated by the hexagonal horse **engine house**, slated with fine local slates. This in turn was replaced by steam power, the **boiler house** served by tall chimneystack. These and other ranges, including **stables**, are built around a hollow square. The high domed silage storage towers are amongst the 20th-century additions to this interesting complex.

Square of Sibster, steading with kiln (r), and ramped barn with boiler house chimneystack (l)

NOSS HEAD, CASTLE GIRNIGOE AND CASTLE SINCLAIR

The long sweep of Sinclair's Bay, terminated by Noss Head, is ringed with both ruined and restored castles, some splendidly sited on precarious clifftops.

Noss Head Lighthouse, 1849, Alan Stevenson
Short circular tower with corbelled balcony enclosed by cast-iron railing. Standard Egyptian-style keepers' houses, also 1849, fronted by courtyard paved with local flagstones, the complex enclosed by rubble stone dyke. Low rubble steading with stable and gighouse.

Above *Noss Head Lighthouse.*
Right *Egyptian style keepers' cottages, Noss Head Lighthouse*

The great stronghold of Girnigoe Castle ... was the last of our Caithness castles to be built on a precipitous cliff-top. Erected sometime between 1476 and 1496 by William, 2nd Sinclair Earl, it was at the time completely impregnable. The promontory on which it stands had been cut away from the mainland both at its base and half way along by great ditches ... Girnigoe remained the seat of five successive earls ... Besieged (c.1690) it was taken and partly destroyed (for the first time in Caithness) by the use of firearms or artillery.
D Omand (ed), *The New Caithness Book*, 1989, p.163

18 **Castle Girnigoe**, from late 15th century and **Castle Sinclair**, 1607 (a separate building within the complex)
Perched dramatically on the cliff edge near Noss Head, amongst the most spectacular fortress remains in northern Scotland. Though ruinous, sufficient remains to give a realistic impression of these remarkable castles. Girnigoe, a stronghold rising four storeys high above vaulted basement, exploits every inch of a high, narrow cliff promontory. The castle was generously supplied with windows set within moulded jambs while the first-floor hall was once lit by a canted oriel, corbelled out from the

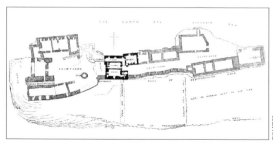

Ground plan, Castle Girnigoe and Castle Sinclair

sheer wallface, from which there was a spectacular panorama of sea and cliffs. Castle Girnigoe is separated by a moat from Castle Sinclair and by protective ditches to landward. Castle Sinclair was apparently built to provide additional, perhaps more comfortable, accommodation than available in Girnigoe, though its ruinous state makes a clear understanding of the building difficult.

Left Castle Sinclair (r) and Castle Girnigoe (l) from Cordiner's North of Scotland *and Smith's* Galic Antiquities. *Above Castle Girnigoe (r) and Castle Sinclair (l)*

ACKERGILL AND WESTER
Ackergill Tower, late 15th/early 16th century, remodelled 1851-2, David Bryce
Tall, five-storey tower house with crenellated wallhead corbelled round angle bartizans. At the rear square bartizans overlook the sea, projecting from east and west corners. The tower house was radically remodelled in baronial style by David Bryce who inserted the arched doorway ornamented with cabled moulded hoodmould and knot terminals, a hallmark of his work in Caithness. He also added the gabled caphouse to the original flat rooftop, originally an admirable lookout platform, besides the drawing-room wing projecting at the east and low service area at west gable. The interior, too, is largely Bryce; a heavy oak staircase leads to the former first-

To the west of **Castle Sinclare** *(sic) ... stands the Castle of Airigill the ancient mansion house of the Earls Marshall, when the Keiths were proprietors of the Baronie of Airigill, a strong house and yet in repair, and betwixt that and the sea is a good new house lately built, both now belonging to the family Hempriggs.* c.1726, MacFarlane's *Geographical Collections*, i, pub.1906. The lands of Ackergill belonged to the Cheynes, passing to the Keiths of Inverugie (Peterhead, Aberdeenshire) c.1350. Acquired by the Dunbars of Hempriggs in 1699, remaining within that family until the 1980s. The description quoted above suggests that an earlier castle was still *in situ* in 1726.

Keiss Bay and Ackergill Tower

floor hall converted into a dining room, with panelling and barrel-vaulted plaster ceiling. Long walls flank the castle, protecting the grounds from salt winds and host to summer flowers. Ackergill Tower is now a conference/hospitality centre.

Ackergill Tower dovecotes, 18th century
Pair of *lectern* models (single-pitch roofs) sited in front of Ackergill Tower; only the eastern building contains dovecote accommodation with 1800 nesting boxes tiered up the walls. The use of the western cote is obscure, though the presence of a small mural hearth suggests a henhouse (see pp.59 & 103).

Ackergill Mains farm steading, from mid-19th century
Imposing range remarkable for pair of tall chimneys, erected at different times, which served boilers producing steam power to motivate threshing and other mechanical farm tasks. The handsome farm buildings were innovatory for their generous provision of steam power besides size and quality of construction.

Top *Ackergill Tower, c.1820, William Daniell.* Top right *Ackergill Tower, 1994.* Middle *Ackergill Tower from shore.* Above *Dovecotes, Ackergill Tower.* Right *Ackergill Mains farm steading*

Leet

Leet

Beaton

Beaton

Left *Swiney House, near Lybster.*
Top *Forse Castle and the Latheron
coastline.* Middle *Berriedale Church
of Scotland.* Above *The 'Duke's
Candlesticks', Berriedale*

49

RCAHMS

Beaton

Beaton

Beaton

Beaton

Beaton

Top *Hempriggs House.* Middle *Buldoo Bell Tower.* Above *Cooperage, Wick Harbour: herring barrels in the making, 1978; workshop contents now in Wick Heritage Centre.* Top left *Orange algae brings brilliant colour to a local slate roof.* Middle left *Longhouse, Roadside Croft, Thrumster. The ruinous far section was the house, now replaced by a modern bungalow.* Bottom left *Main Street, Lybster*

Beaton

Beaton

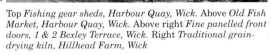

Beaton

Top *Fishing gear sheds, Harbour Quay, Wick.* Above *Old Fish Market, Harbour Quay, Wick.* Above right *Fine panelled front doors, 1 & 2 Bexley Terrace, Wick.* Right *Traditional grain-drying kiln, Hillhead Farm, Wick*

Beaton

Below *Cast-iron railing, George
Street, Wick.* Bottom *Mausoleum,
Stroma*

Top *Caithness General Hospital, Wick.* Middle *Canisbay
Parish Church.* Above *Box bed, Stroma, photographed in
1978*

Ackergillshore old lifeboat house, 1878,
William Brims
The earliest extant lifeboat house in the
Highlands. Simple rubble boatshed with
charming original RNLI roundels depicting a
crew in sou'westers pulling at the oars of a
lifeboat. The ferro-concrete slipway of 1910 was
the first of its kind to be constructed in Great
Britain. Early 19th-century single-chambered
icehouse built into bank by slipway.

Left *Ackergillshore old lifeboat
house, with salmon cobble; note
roundels left and right of entrance.*
Above *Worn, weathered roundel
Ackergillshore old lifeboat house*

A lifeboat was established at Wick
as early as 1848; when called, it was
drawn by horses to Ackergill to
rescue ships in distress in Sinclairs'
Bay. After the sinking of the *Emelie*
in the bay, on 23 December 1876,
with loss of life, a lifeboat was
established at Ackergillshore in
1878, manned by local volunteers.
The lifeboat house was designed by
Mr (William) Brims, architect, Wick,
constructed on land donated by Mr
F Duff-Dunbar of Hempriggs and
Ackergill Tower. The boathouse
carries the original ceramic roundels
of the RNLI. The station was closed
in 1932.
Jeff Morris, *The Story of the Wick
and Ackergill Lifeboats*, 1984

Bridge of Wester, 1830-40, after
Thomas Telford
Designed to span the Wick River at Watten but
not executed; the drawings were later utilised
for a bridge spanning the Wester River.
Imposing twin-arched rubble structure with
slender central pier and triangular cutwaters;
now bypassed.

LYTH
19 **Barrock House**, largely mid-19th century,
incorporating earlier work
Rambling and pleasant, crowstepped, gabled
and asymmetrical mansion with tall
chimneystacks and canted bay windows: re-
used datestone of 1632 over main entrance
recalls ownership by a branch of the Sinclair
family from 1631. At the rear there is a small
18th-century house, relegated as service wing.
The wooded policies and tree-lined drive are

Williams Brims, 1820-1901, a
native of Watten who carried on
business first as a carpenter and
afterwards as an architect in Wick.
Obituary, *John o'Groat Journal,*
29 March 1901

Barrock House

uncommon in Caithness; they provide welcome shelter. Mid-19th-century Mains Farm **steading** with symmetrical frontage, the arched entrance under a crenellated tower. The type is common in north-east Scotland but unusual in Caithness.

Lyth Old School and Schoolhouse, late 19th century
Gabled range within walled enclosure now serving a new use as a thriving arts centre. *Open for exhibitions July-August and for evening performances, April-September*

KEISS

Harbour and fishing store, 1983

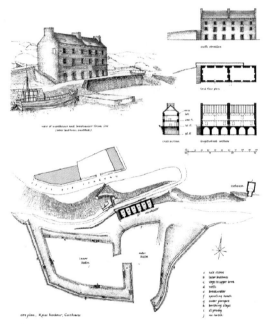

site plan., Keiss harbour, Caithness RCAHMS

Keiss village expanded during the early 19th-century fishing boom. The fine **harbour** (see p.5), with its outer stilling basin, was constructed *c*.1831 by James Bremner, a native of Keiss, shipbuilder and harbour engineer of note (see p.42). The masonry is of excellent quality, some of the coursing laid vertically to counteract the upward pressure of the tidal sea. There is a handsome three-storey **fishing store** beside the quay while the **terrace** of local stone houses on the clifftop above enhances the setting. A gabled **icehouse** is built snugly into a bank by the beach (see p.15). The slot in the

Icehouse, Keiss Harbour

Beaton

gable wall of the old salmon fishers' bothy formerly housed a barometer (see also Lybster): this is approached by a forestair to facilitate examination of a vital aid to seamen before the days of regular radio weather forecasts.

Keiss Church of Scotland, 1827, Thomas Telford Parliamentary T-plan design, with later alterations and interior refurbishing. Original bellcote survives. Former **manse**, also 1827, Thomas Telford. Standard two storey with later rear wing (see p.6). **Free Church**, 1893-5, Mr Barnie, Edinburgh, superintended by William Brims; mechanical Gothic with austere street frontage described as a *handsome Gothic edifice constructed to seat over 400* (*John o'Groat Journal*, 25 August 1893).

Old Keiss Castle, late 16th century Roofless shell standing boldly on the cliff edge: four storeys high with some fine sandstone ashlar detailing, particularly the chequered corbelling beneath turrets and bartizans (see also Brims, p.93). The castle was superseded in 1755 by **Keiss House**, a symmetrical three-storey mansion, immediately fulfilling the fashionable role of romantic ruin enhancing the landscape. The wheel of architectural fashion came full circle 100 years later with the baronial revival. Keiss House became **Keiss Castle** engulfed in extensive castellated additions in 1860 to a design by David Bryce. The entrance has his characteristic cabled hoodmould, there is a crenellated tower and angle bartizans: long windows overlook the gardens and coast, the baronial structure crisply smart with black-and-white paintwork.

Keiss Church of Scotland

David Bryce, 1803-76, architect in Edinburgh; pupil and assistant of William Burn, partner from 1844 (see p.84). Bryce excelled in the Scottish Baronial Revival style and, like Burn, had an extensive country-house practice.

Below *Keiss Castle with old Keiss Castle in background*. Bottom *Doorpiece, Keiss Castle*. Left *Old Keiss Castle*

Top Nybster broch with sculpture by John Nicolson. Above Keiss Baptist Chapel and manse, Nybster

Summerbank, Nybster, early 19th century Plain farmhouse decorated with stone carvings and statues by John Nicolson (*c*.1843-1934) a sculptor of local repute who crowded farming, geology and archaeology into a long and busy life. **Nybster broch** (see p.10), much decorated with Nicolson carvings including memorial to Sir F Tress Barry, local laird and archaeologist. Former Nybster School, late 19th century, now the **Northlands Viking Centre**, houses work by Nicolson, the interior designed by his architect nephew, Jack Sutherland. *Open during summer months.* More work by John Nicolson decorates the **Auckingill Hall**, built for the use of returning servicemen from the First World War.

Keiss Baptist Chapel, Nybster, 19th century Plain and undistinguished but notable as successor to the first Baptist Chapel in Scotland, established in 1750. Commemorative plaque to the founder and first pastor, Sir William Sinclair of Keiss a *zealous Anabaptist* (who) *... made some proselytes amongst his tenants.* Simple 19th-century **manse** neighbours the chapel.

FRESWICK

On the north side *of the house (Freswick) a brook or burn runs into the sea, over which is a bridge of one arch over against the gate. At the further end whereof is a lately erected chappel (sic) with a vault for burying in the place where ane old popish chappel stood that in very late times was much resorted to by ignorant and superstitious people who by devotions and offerings made to the St (sic) expected recovery of their health.*
Entry of *c*.1726 from MacFarlane's *Geographical Collections*, i, p.153

Freswick has been occupied for around 2000 years. There is a cliff-edge broch site between Freswick House and Buchollie while the bay was the site of a Norse settlement. A farm at Freswick, situated on the links beside the shore, is mentioned in the *Orkneyinga Saga*: excavations have also revealed evidence of extensive Norse fishing activity. **Lambaborg** or **Freswick Castle**, the predecessor of **Buchollie Castle**, is said to have been the 12th-century stronghold of Sweyne Asliefson, a Norse pirate, whose exploits are also chronicled in the *Saga*. The lands of Freswick passed to the Mowats, who renamed the castle Buchollie after their Aberdeenshire estate; in 1661 they sold the property to the Sinclairs of Rattar. Beautiful Freswick Bay is fringed with a sandy beach and links, richly strewn with wild flowers in summertime, and enclosed by rocky headlands: no wonder it has attracted generations of settlers and landowners.

Buchollie Castle, 13th century Fragmentary remains of tower with battered base and courtyard perched on a narrow rocky peninsula to south of Freswick Bay; it exploits every corner of this impregnable site 100 ft or so above the sea. Access was through a sunken passage in the neck of land linking the mainland.

Freswick House, late 18th century, probably incorporating earlier core
Sited on a rise overlooking the crescent-shaped sandy beach of Freswick Bay, successor to Buchollie Castle. Impressively tall, handsome, five-storey, regularly fronted mansion with projecting north front stair tower. The main doorway is in the south elevation, at first-floor level reached by a flight of steps. This south front is enclosed within a high-walled courtyard accessed through an archway: the south side of the inner court is filled by a substantial early 18th-century crowstepped barn. There was a house here before 1726, badly damaged 50 years later by a thunderstorm which *threw down a chimney top, and rent the wall from top to bottom, besides damaging the greatest part of the windows.* By 1791 it was a *modern building, sufficiently commodious and elegant.* This *modern building* of Freswick House was probably a rebuild and regularisation of the 17th-century house, generously provided with symmetrical fenestration. Freswick House,

Freswick Castle (Buchollie) *is seated on a narrow rock projecting into the sea, with just room enough for it to stand on: the access to it while the draw-bridge was in being, was over a deep chasm cut thro' the little isthmus that connected it to the main land. These dreadfull situations are strongly expressive of the jealous and wretched condition of the tyrant owners.*
Thomas Pennant, A Tour of Scotland in 1769, 3rd edn, 1774

neither truly tower house nor conventional 18th-century mansion, is a splendid enigma in a sublime setting. It is approached over a single-span **bridge**, also known to have existed by 1726; in the wide masonry abutment there is a small mural chamber, the *Cruelty Hoose,* allegedly used as a prison.

Freswick House dovecote, probably 17th century
Domed rubble *beehive doocot* with smoke-blackened interior and (unusually) two doorways, indications of alteration and re-use as a drying or smoking kiln (respectively grain

Left Freswick House. Below Freswick House dovecote

The name **John o'Groats** is said to be derived from Jan de Grot, one of three brothers who came to Caithness from Holland in 1496. They rented land at Duncansby from the Earl of Caithness for which they paid a penny rent plus three measures of malt. It is also said that John ran a ferry to Orkney, charging a groat (fourpence) as fare. Tradition has it that Jan de Grot had an annual reunion with his seven sons and that at one of these the young men quarrelled about precedence at table. The tactful de Grot had an eight-sided room made and fitted with an octagonal table, reputed to have survived into the early 1800s. The family is commemorated by a carved stone slab in Canisbay Church.

or fish). **Mausoleum**, *c.*1700, roofless rectangle constructed on site of former St Madden's chapel.

JOHN O'GROATS, DUNCANSBY HEAD AND HUNA

John o'Groats, much frequented by visitors, is also the ferry terminal for South Ronaldsay, Orkney. Together with Huna and neighbouring townships the undulating landscape is thickly scattered with small cottages, bungalows and crofts. Duncansby Head commands a spectacular panorama south over steep cliffs and the Stacks of Duncansby and north to the Pentland Firth and Orkney. In spring the short turf is bright with wild flowers including blue squill, while pink thrift clings to rocky ledges.

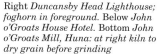

Right Duncansby Head Lighthouse; foghorn in foreground. Below John o'Groats House Hotel. Bottom John o'Groats Mill, Huna: at right kiln to dry grain before grinding

Duncansby Head Lighthouse, 1924, D A Stevenson
Tapering square tower with crenellated wallhead and polygonal lantern; large, separately mounted foghorn.

John o'Groats House Hotel, 1875, Thomson Sinclair
Rambling two-storey hostelry dominated by three-stage octagonal corner tower topped by stumpy slated spire, the plan form perpetuating the *de Grot* building legend. The octagonal theme is repeated in the contemporary design of the **First o' Last** shop close to the late 19th-century masonry pier.

John o'Groats Mill, Huna
Two corn mills, the larger, 1750, was originally a threshing mill but was rebuilt in 1901 as a corn mill. This reversed the function of the smaller mill, 1846, which then became the threshing mill. The former has a tall double-vented kiln, the mill motivated by an overshot wheel. Both mills share the same lade (mill stream). **Cromwell Bridge**, allegedly mid-17th century and constructed by Cromwellian

troops: elegant single-span rubble bridge spanning the mill burn.

KIRKSTYLE AND CANISBAY
Canisbay Parish Church, Kirkstyle, medieval origins
The church, on high ground overlooking Gills Bay and the Pentland Firth, has for centuries served as a landmark for shipping. Continuously rebuilt and altered in 17th, early 18th and 19th centuries, it is cruciform and whitewashed, the chunky square tower capped by saddleback roof adorned with apex ball finials (see p.6). South frontage is lit by long 19th-century windows breaking the wallhead under gablets with entry through the former south aisle, lit by a traceried window and housing a tombstone to the Groat (originally de Grot) family erected in 1568 (restored by John Nicolson). Galleried interior, east and west galleries supported by slender cast-iron columns. Pilastered and corniced north gallery, formerly the Sinclair of Mey laird's loft. Eighteenth/early 19th-century layout with pews grouped around pulpit sited against south wall (colour page 52).

Above *Grot (Groat) tombstone, Canisbay Parish Church*. Left *Canisbay Parish Church*

Donald Grot, *sone to Johne Grot laid me heir April XIII day 1568 M.D.L. Lewys and Donald Grot and his gonaield lad and thaar faorbears of Donald whouse God cald me ye XIII day of April. Anno Dominy MDL 1568.*
Inscription on Grot (Groat) tombstone, Canisbay Church

The surrounding **burial ground** contains a remarkable collection of tombstones, including one carved by the local sculptor, John Nicolson of Nybster (see p.56), in memory of his mother who died in 1868.

The Old Manse, Canisbay, late 18th century
Usual two-storey, three-window proportions but the original sash-and-case windows have been replaced by inappropriate modern glazing. As was customary, the manse was provided with **walled garden**, **gighouse**, **stable**, **byre**, **barn** with **kiln** (now removed) and a service **cottage** with nesting boxes for hens set in the outside gable, warmed by the chimney flue. Warm hens are happy hens, and happy hens lay eggs! The

Above *Cast-iron porch, Canisbay.*
Right *Stroma from the air, revealing
an intensively farmed landscape*

south-facing garden wall has unusual
semicircular beeboles, mural alcoves to house
circular straw beehives. Beeboles are more
commonly square or a continuous shelf. **West
Canisbay** is a handsome late 18th-century
farmhouse with regular frontage and wings set
back at each gable.

Canisbay post office, 19th century
Traditional pair of two-storey houses, one of
which has a delicate, decorative cast-iron
porch, marred by later repairs.

STROMA

*The Harbour, Stroma, 1904: in the
foreground the boat which brought
the doctor over from the mainland;
people in Sunday best gather to talk*

The island of **Stroma**, clearly visible from
Canisbay, was identified in the sagas as
Straumey, the Island in the Stream. By 1659 it
had been purchased by John Kennedy of
Carnmuch (Kairnmuch), Aberdeenshire, who
built a mansion with a garden of herbs at the
north end of the island besides a family
mausoleum on the medieval chapel site and
burial ground at the south east. The island was
intensively farmed, the chequer-board pattern
of small, dyked fields most evident from the air.
The population peaked in 1901 to 375,
gradually declining and finally abandoned in
the 1960s. The cottage homes stand empty,
silhouetted on the skyline when viewed from
the mainland. These were well built, mostly
with finely carpentered internal furnishings
including box beds with panelled fronts detailed
as ships' bunks. This vernacular detailing
probably reflects the influence of Stroma's sea-
going inhabitants, who were well known for
their excellent seamanship (colour page 52).

Mausoleum, 1677
Stands in the **burial ground** at the extreme
south-east of the island. Square with roofless
pigeon loft in first floor above. The building,
dated 1677, is initialled I K for John Kennedy
(I synonymous with J, not introduced into
alphabet by this date) (colour p.52). **Lighthouse**,
1896, D A Stevenson, is now automatic. A
circular, 60ft (27.43m) high tower with a terrace
of three single-storey cottages, sited at Swilkie
Point (*Swilkie*, Norse for whirlpool).

Baptist Chapel, 1877, William Brims and
Church of Scotland (succeeding earlier
church), 1878. Both tall, gaunt buildings.

*An island belongs to this parish,
called Stroma, in which there is a
vault where they bury, built by one
Kennedy of Carnmuch. The coffins
are laid on stools above ground. But
the vault being on the sea edge, and
the rapid tides of the Pentland Firth
running by it, there is such a saltish
air continually, as has converted the
bodies into mummies: insomuch,
that one Murdo Kennedy, son of
Carnmuch, is said to beat the drum
on his father's belly.*
Alexander Pope in Thomas Pennant,
A Tour of Scotland in 1769, 3rd edn,
1774

BRABSTERMIRE

20 **Brabster Castle**, *c*.1650
Surviving gable wall of a former tower-house is
incorporated in a tall corn-drying **kiln**
prominent on the hillside from the road and
even from Freswick Bay (colour page 71). Long
roofless 19th-century cruck-framed **barn** to the
rear measuring approximately 67ft x 19ft (21m
x 6m). No cruck trusses survive, though three
mural cruck slots reveal the original
construction whereby paired cruck blades or
couples (Scots) supported the weight of the roof.
The tower-house was succeeded by
Brabstermire House, a sturdy, traditional,
18th-century, two-storey Caithness laird's
house, less prestigious but more comfortable
than the windswept tower. Later this became a
farmhouse, now disused and incorporated
within the farmsteading complex.

*Brabster Castle, the residence of
the Sinclairs (of Brabster), is old,
and situate in the most inland part
of the parish (Canisbay).*
Nicholas Carlisle, *Topographical
Dictionary of Scotland*, i, 1813

Historic Scotland

RCAHMS

*Above Brabster Castle; gable end
and kiln. Left Brabstermire House,
c.1970 before conversion as farm
steading c.1990*

*The Town and House of Brabster
belonging to George Sinclare (sic) of
Brabster stands three miles NW
from Freswick, two miles SW from
the church, and two miles SE from
the House of Mey.*
Early 18th-century description from
MacFarlane's *Geographical
Collections*, i, p.153

MEY AND HARROW

21 **Castle of Mey**, probably 1566-72,
later additions
The castle, which enjoys a commanding position
over the Pentland Firth and Orkney, was built
by George, 4th Earl of Caithness, as a plain
four-storey tower with flat roof and angle

National Galleries of Scotland

RCAHMS

Above *Barrogill Castle (Castle of Mey), c.1825, William Daniell.* Right *Castle of Mey after alterations and additions by William Burn and subsequently Hugh Macdonald for HM The Queen Mother*

Castle Arms Hotel

Beaton

bartizans (turrets). In due course a slightly lower wing was added at the west and it was renamed Barrogill Castle. In 1819 William Burn baronialised the building; he removed the conical roofs from the bartizans, giving them a more baronial style with crenellations and added the entrance porch, besides other work which does not survive. The castle was purchased in 1953 by HM The Queen Mother who reverted it to the original name of Castle of Mey and for whom further alterations were made by Hugh Macdonald (Sinclair Macdonald & Son). Her Majesty's coat of arms above the first-floor windows was carved by Hew Lorimer.

Barrogill Mains, *c.*1840
Formerly Mains Farm (home farm) to Barrogill Castle (Castle of Mey). L-plan, two-storey house with wide three-bay frontage, piended roof with flared copes to ridge chimneystacks. Two-pane windows replace original lying-pane (horizontal) glazing. Original recessed entrance now masked by modern flat-roofed porch.

Castle Arms Hotel (formerly Berriedale Arms Inn), simple two-storey building enhanced by fine cast-iron work: the porch is embellished by decorative cresting and crowned with crowing cock, the dormers by tall thistle finials. Former **Drill Hall**, 1875, gabled and bargeboarded; its domestic character belies the military role.

Harrow Harbour (Phillips' Harbour), early 19th century
Sited in a cleft below the Castle of Mey, approached through a gully yellow with primroses in springtime. Curved masonry pier linked to quay, repaired in concrete 1978-9. Early 19th-century vaulted **icehouse** built into a bank indicates former salmon-fishing activity. Roofless engine shed housed steam-driven saws

used to trim flagstones. Opposite the engine shed is a much-overgrown tramway, apparently used to bring the flagstones from the quarry for trimming and then on to the harbour for export. Datestone on engine house reads *1871 RC MEY*. This was one of the many industrialised sites, complete with up-to-date transport and mechanisation, associated with the flagstone industry, for which Castletown and Thurso were paramount (see pp.67 & 76).

Above *Datestone, engine house, Harrow Harbour.* Left *Flagstone dressing (r) engine house (l). The chimney appears to have been heightened to increase draw; this extension no longer exists though the squat stack survives*

James, 14th Earl of Caithness, 1821-81, was a *pioneer of mechanical locomotion.* He was the inventor of a *steam carriage* in which he drove from Inverness to Barrogill Castle (Castle of Mey) in 1860. This was *in the form of a phaeton* (horse-drawn carriage) with a water tank holding 170 gallons of water and a boiler requiring 1 cwt for every 20 miles. The Earl also invented the car wash for cleaning American railway cars (*Caithness Courier*, 1 Feb. 1873). He died in New York, 21 March 1881. His first wife was Louisa Phillips, after whom the harbour at Harrow was named.

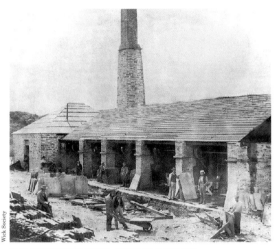

SCARFSKERRY AND RATTAR

Scarfskerry and Rattar are two coastal linear settlements, the former close to a deep coastal cleft with pier.

Ferry House, Scarfskerry, from early 19th century
Overlooks the bay and the Pentland Firth and Orkney, not very different from the plain two-storey dwelling drawn by William Daniell in 1813. **The Haven** also sited above the bay, a pair of cottages modernised with traditional materials by Lyndall Leet in 1984 & 1987. The roof has been innovatively heightened, incorporating a canted glazed gablet commanding a panoramic outlook across the firth (colour page 69). Fine drystone dykes enclose the garden.

Rattar House, early 19th century
Two-storey, symmetrical H-plan house – grandly described in 1813 as *Seat of the Earls of Caithness*, to which the present house is probably a successor.

HAM AND BARROCK

Ham

Coastal inlet with ruinous harbour once providing a reasonably safe anchorage. **Ham Mill**, probably an 18th-century warehouse or girnel converted to mill in early 19th century. The tall frontage is lit by symmetrical five-window fenestration, the outer windows paired in *c.*1730 manner while the east gable facing the shore is well served with hoist doors. Outgoing grain and other goods were stored in girnals awaiting shipment and incoming cargoes kept pending collection. Rents paid in kind (mainly corn) would have been deposited here by tenants and realised for cash by the landlord through sale at home and abroad.

Right *Ham Mill and mill pond.*
Below *Ham Farmhouse.* Bottom
Barrock Free Church

Ham Farmhouse, 18th century, is sited on a rise overlooking the inlet and mill pond. Conventional two storeys with central wallhead gablet, later extended at right and the windows enlarged.

22 **Barrock Free Church** (disused), 1844 Large double-aisled church, its size indicative of the strength and effort of the Free Church break-away. Funded by local effort, the congregation could only afford a *felt* roof in 1844 but by 1849 had paid for slating.

DUNNET

Dunnet Head projects like a great whale back into the Pentland Firth with Dunnet village tucked into its shelter on the north side of deep, sandy-shored Dunnet Bay (colour page 70).

Parish Church, medieval core, tower probably 17th century, north aisle 1837
Simple, low, whitewashed T-plan church enclosed within a walled burial ground overlooking Dunnet Bay. A strong, evocative building that, like neighbouring Canisbay, has dignified the site since medieval times. Long and low with a squat saddleback tower at the west gable accommodating a doorway in the

The Revd Timothy Pont, *c.*1560-*c.*1625/30, cartographer, mathematician and minister of Dunnet, 1601-14. Pont compiled an atlas of Scotland diligently surveying the equivalent of two counties each summer between 1584 and 1596. The *minutely and elegantly penned* originals are in the National Library of Scotland; they were the basis of the 49 maps of Scotland in Volume V of the splendid Blaeu's *Atlas Novus*, 1654.

Left *Parish Church.* Above *Former manse*

base and diminutive lights. The construction sequence is surprisingly difficult, the tower may have been constructed at two different periods. The plain interior retains its traditional layout with box pews and pulpit against the south wall. There is a **mural memorial** to its most celebrated incumbent, the Revd Timothy Pont. The **burial ground** is tightly packed with tombs from 17th century onwards. Former **manse**, *c*.1840; two storeys, with centre recessed bay with corniced doorway flanked by slightly advanced and gabled outer bays. Nicely executed in well-tooled stone.

Mary Ann's Cottage, Westside Croft, Single-storey, linear croft complex with whitewashed rubble cottage in centre flanked by byre, stable, cartshed and barn on one side and store and henhouse on the other, each of different builds and with varied roofing including graded Caithness slates, *sheddies* (large flagstones), corrugated iron and

I have known this croft for a long time. It is in its own right a most important social document. It incorporates in its layouts and fittings a natural blend of the old and the new, showing how innovations and more modern concepts gradually displace or replace the old. In terms of field layout and details like the tethering of animals and the siting of plantcots for cabbage propagating on adjacent ground, there are rare pointers to the older, pre-improvement community system that prevailed throughout much of Scotland. It can be used therefore, to interpret both the past and the more recent present, especially if it can be preserved with all its contents intact.
Professor Alexander Fenton, Director, European Ethnological Research Centre

Below *Mary Ann's Cottage.* Bottom *Mary Ann's Cottage, with Northern Gate House on skyline*

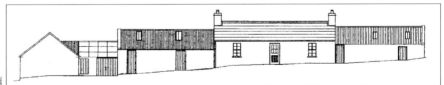

Top *Box bed, Mary Ann's Cottage.*
Above *Northern Gate House*

corrugated asbestos. In front is a small walled
vegetable patch. The croft was worked in
traditional manner by James and Mary Ann
Calder until *c.*1990. Now cared for by the
Caithness Heritage Trust; *open during summer
months*

Northern Gate House, *c.*1903,
Sinclair Macdonald
Scottish Renaissance; plain, white-harled
house sited high on Dunnet Head with a
spectacular outlook. The pedimented dormers
breaking the wallhead decorated with heavy
scroll or cavetto skewputts, chunky angle
bartizan turrets, angle stair tower and tall
chimneystacks give a baronial flavour to this
windswept landmark. The house was built by
Admiral Sir Alexander Sinclair of Dunbeath
Castle, allegedly as a shooting lodge for
himself and brother naval officers when
serving in the area. Originally it was named
Dwarwick House (it stands above Dwarwick
Head).

Dunnet Head Lighthouse, 1830-3,
Robert Stevenson
Short circular, corbelled tower clasped at base
by a single-storey, semicircular service room;
fronted by simple flat-roofed lightkeepers'
houses, the complex within paved yard
enclosed by rubble walls. Large directable
foghorn mounted on stumpy base. Dunnet
Light is the most northerly mainland
lighthouse in Scotland. Building materials and
stores were ferried by sea from **Brough** (locally
Brug), a sheltered inlet with **slipway** and
single-storey **store** with the door lintel
inscribed *2 miles 3 Qr. and 11 yds from the
LIGHTHOUSE 1830* (colour page 69).

Top *Inscribed panel on lighthouse
store, Brough.* Above *Lighthouse
store, Brough.* Right *Dunnet Head
Lighthouse; foghorn in foreground*

CASTLETOWN AND OLRIG

Castletown, from *c.*1802

A linear village associated with the local flagstone industry on the south side of Dunnet Bay, approached from the east through a wooded glade, a rare sylvan experience in Caithness. Castletown was planned as early as 1802 by Sheriff James Traill though it did not operate fully until 1825. Soil heaps litter the quarry area, now arranged as a *quarry trail*. More flagstone quarries were at Stonegun and Weydale, on high ground to the south-west from where a small (horse-drawn) tramway transported flags from Weydale to Thurso. It is said that the horse was a passenger on the downward journey, contentedly chewing the contents of his nosebag but harnessed to the trucks for the long haul back!

The surrounding countryside is largely agricultural while Dunnet Head dominates the coastal landscape. The parish is Olrig, the ruinous **church** sited in the burial ground a couple of miles north of Castletown.

Former quarriers' **cottages** in the main street built of thin, spent flagstones. Some interesting local authority **housing** with recessed porches, designed by James Henderson, *c.*1950 (see p.8).

Old Castletown Church (disused), 1840, David Cousin

Once imposing Gothic building with a tower but sadly down at heel, sited more conveniently for Castletown village than old Olrig church a couple of miles to the south. Both superseded by **Olrig Parish Church**, 1913, former United Free Church: sturdy, with asymmetrical gable bellcote and faintly

Castlehill House

James Traill, 1758-1847, lawyer and Sheriff-Depute of Caithness, was the energetic landlord of Olrig Parish and Castletown. He was deeply involved in agricultural improvements, encouraged the growing of flax, built flax and grain mills and industrialised the flagstone industry for which he constructed the harbour. Though flagstone had been quarried earlier, it was from 1825 that the industry really expanded, employing 100 quarriers rising to 500 by 1900 in the Castletown quarries alone. Caithness flagstones were used for paving all over Great Britain and exported widely, including to New Zealand and South America. Castlehill, Traill's house in Castletown, was burnt down in 1970.

Olrig Parish Church

Top *War memorial.* Above *Castletown public hall & reading room*

A public hall and reading room, a munificent gift from the late Miss Margaret Traill to the people of Olrig, was opened with appropriate ceremony on New Year's Day, 1867, in the village of Castletown. The length of the building is 80 feet and the breadth 28, and it has a beautiful and large oval window. The building is a boon and ornament to the locality.
J T Calder, *History of Caithness*, 1887, p.365

art nouveau street gable. The plan was standard to the UF church, supervised and adapted by Sinclair Macdonald. The plain interior is illuminated and cheered by clear quarried windows with modest colourful art nouveau decoration, larger, more ornate versions of the same design incorporating the burning bush and a dove flanking the pulpit, all by Oscar Paterson, Glasgow, installed in 1913. Neighbouring gabled **manse**, 1916, also Sinclair Macdonald.

Free Church, 1843 (disused, now workshop/store): usual Caithness double-gabled, double-aisled Free Church fronted by centre porch. Some margined, lying-pane glazing with delicate astragals survives (see p.6).

War memorial, 1925, Percy Portsmouth Tall block of pale Leggat sandstone with recess in upper portion housing a bronze figure representing *Repentance.*

Castletown public hall & reading room, 1866
Gabled and asymmetrical, graced with an unusual large mullioned bay window flooding the reading room with light: presented to the village by Miss Margaret Traill, daughter of Sheriff Traill, whose initials are inscribed above the main door. Sadly disused.

Castletown Mill, dated 1818 or 1819, very large, disused cornmill, its size reflecting the richness of the agricultural hinterland.

Borgie House, 1860-70
Substantial, two-storey, former Church of Scotland manse with asymmetrical frontage standing apart from the village within walled garden.

Castlehill
An early 19th-century mansion stood within walled policies backing on to the shore. Large mains farm complex with mill, extensive steading and dairy in process of restoration by The Leet Rodgers Practice, the dairy as an *interpretative centre* for the quarry site.
Castlehill Quarries with a small, neat conical **windmill**, designed to pump away surplus water. Quarry area flanked by

Middle *Oat harvest on a Dunnet croft.* Above *Drill Hall, Castletown*

Top *Brough pier, from where materials were taken to Dunnet Head in 1830 to construct the lighthouse.* Middle *The Haven, Scarfskerry: modern ridge oriel commands coastal panorama.* Above *High Street, Thurso: painting by D B Keith, 1950. The houses have subsequently been demolished*

Watson

McKean

McKean

The Highland Council

Top *Castletown, Dunnet Bay and Dunnet Head.* Above
*Topographical print of Thurso by John Warner Scott,
Architect, 1860, Thurso Library.* Above left *Old Brewery,
Thurso.* Left *Old St Peter's Church (l), The White House (r),
Thurso*

Opposite: clockwise from top left *Pentland House; Brabster
Castle, Brabstermire; Forss Mill and bridge; Olrig House gate
lodge, Castletown*

70

Top *Old Skinnet House.* Above *Flagstone field dykes*

Watson

Beaton

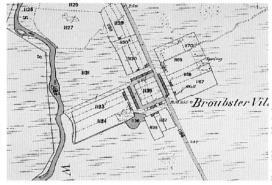

National Library of Scotland

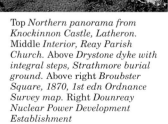

Beaton

Top *Northern panorama from Knockinnon Castle, Latheron.* Middle *Interior, Reay Parish Church.* Above *Drystone dyke with integral steps, Strathmore burial ground.* Above right *Broubster Square, 1870, 1st edn Ordnance Survey map.* Right *Dounreay Nuclear Power Development Establishment*

UKAEA, Dounreay

W Ashley Bartlam

abandoned flagstone dressing sheds and workers' cottages. Now arranged as *quarry trail* with information plaques: *open at all times*

Castlehill Harbour, *c.*1820, James Bremner, with wide paved triangular quay designed to facilitate the handling of bulky flagstones exported by boat.

Beaton

Beaton

Castletown Artillery Battery
Remains of a mid-19th-century artillery bastion on the coast east of the village (map ref: ND 194690), approached by the coastal track or from the main road via Battery Lane. A crescent-shaped, turfed wall with flagstone-faced embrasures, overlooking the firth. Used for training local artillery volunteers. Their **Drill Hall**, *c.*1870, is in the centre of Castletown, a suitably military building of two storeys, with centre wallhead gable and flanking full-height angle turrets with conical roofs (colour page 69).

OLRIG
Old Kirk
Roofless rectangle dated 1633 and 1743 on north-east and south-east skewputts respectively but incorporating medieval fabric;

Beaton

it stands in the **burial ground** with many fine tombs and memorials. By the gate there is a stone basin (?font) dated 1666. Close by the burial ground are the remains of the 18th-century, two-storey **manse**.

Olrig House, mid and late 19th century, with 18th-century core
Sited on a wooded, pastoral slope overlooking Castletown and the Pentland Firth: a dignified mid-19th-century porticoed and pilastered house whose classical frontage contrasts markedly with the *c*.1880 asymmetrical rear. David Bryce drew up a scheme for more alterations in 1859-61, only partially executed. Back of house approached through *c*.1880 courtyard arch enclosed by rear elevation and crowstepped service range, remodelled *c*.1880, together with the rear additions to the main house suggesting the style of Sir James Gowans, Edinburgh.

Right Olrig House. Below Olrig House gate lodge; idiosyncratic treatment of masonry in style of Sir James Gowans. Bottom Bower Parish Church

Olrig House gate lodge, *c*.1880, probably Sir James Gowans; restored *c*.1994, The Leet Rodgers Practice
Delightful with endlessly inventive detailing, bold gables, steeply pitched roof with deep eaves, diminutive oriel window, ribbed and studded front door and angle masonry simulating Scandinavian log-cabin construction in stone (colour page 71).

BOWER
A few miles south of Castletown (B876) is the rural parish of Bower, consisting largely of scattered farms.

Bower Parish Church, *c*.1847-8, William Davidson, alterations by Donald Leed, 1902
Plain rectangular church with two long

windows in north wall: between these would
have stood the pulpit, more usually sited in the
centre of the south elevation giving better light.
The aisled interior was recast to east in 1902
and fitted with handsome pews with scroll
ends; Gothic detailing to pulpit which is
flanked by an unusual wooden screen. **Mural
memorial** to Zachary Pont, minister, 1605-13,
and his wife Margaret, John Knox's second
daughter. Zachary's better-known brother
Timothy, the 16th/17th-century cartographer,
was minister at neighbouring Dunnet. The
remains of the earlier parish **church** stand in
the nearby **burial ground**: probably medieval
but reconstructed in 1718 and 1803. Tall,
gabled, late 19th-century former parish **manse**
completes the loosely knit complex.

*Olrig House gate lodge, bull's eye
window overlooking driveway entrance*

THURSO
The name **Thurso** may be derived from the
Norse god Thor, though the area was never
fully integrated into the Norse world. There
was a settlement there in the 12th century: in
1719 the lands and burgh of Thurso were
acquired by the Sinclairs of Ulbster, the family
subsequently settling at Thurso East.
Old Thurso grew where the River Thurso
flowed into the sea on the east side of Thurso
Bay. Protected by Holborn Head on the west

***Thurso** is but a Burgh of Barony …
(It) export(s) Beef, tallow, Hides,
Butter, Cheese, Meal, Bear (bere,
type of barley), Plaidins, Some Oyl,
wild Leather and Furres, Salmon,
white fish and slates; and in return
Wine, Brandy, Salt, Lime, Cloth,
Silks and Cramery-Ware.*
Early 18th-century description of
Thurso from MacFarlane's
Geographical Collections, iii, p.86

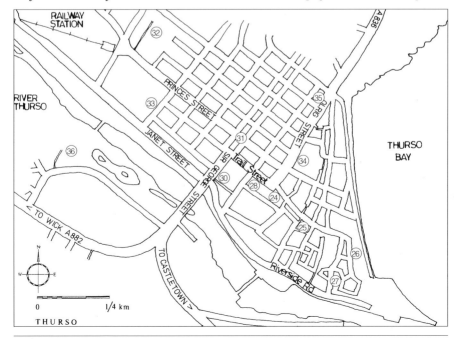

Old St Peter's Church, note tracery in early 17th-century south gable window

and Clairdon Head at the east, the bay offered relative (on the exposed Pentland Firth) shelter (colour page 70). The random street pattern reflects the irregular growth of the medieval old town, particularly close to the curving High Street. Much of this pattern survives, though new housing has changed some of the old layout, and it contrasts markedly with the formal grid pattern of early 19th-century expansion. The new town of Thurso was laid out by Sir John Sinclair of Ulbster in 1798, the area bounded by Rose Street, Olrig Street, Traill Street and Janet Street (named after his mother) more or less as he planned it. Here a regular layout of parallel wide principal streets lined with houses fronting the pavement is bisected by narrow communicating lanes.

Thurso was the commercial centre of the north, the principal port on the south side of the Pentland Firth. A wide range of goods was imported and exported, in the 19th century, the latter including large quantities of Caithness flagstone, an industry which dwindled away in the 1920s. Fish-curing was also an important activity. The town has expanded greatly on all sides, particularly from the 1950s with the influx of employees from the atomic energy station at Dounreay.

Old Thurso

Rotterdam Street, Burgh Chambers at right

Rotterdam Street and High Street are the main thoroughfares in the old town: the name Rotterdam is an obvious pointer to extensive trading links with the Low Countries and elsewhere in Europe. Some much-altered 17th- and 18th-century houses line these sinuous streets though the public buildings are 19th century. There is extensive sympathetic local authority housing in the old town, some terraces incorporating earlier building, the overall layout by Sir Frank Mears. Until 1975 Thurso was its own planning authority, the burgh housing development projected before 1975 though completed later, with the architects concerned aware of local building traditions.

24 **Burgh Chambers** (former National Bank of Scotland), Rotterdam Street, c.1860, style of Matthews & Laurie, Inverness
Plain regularly fronted building with corniced doorpiece. The street gives way to **High Street**
25 (colour page 69) with the **Town Hall**, 1870, J Russell Mackenzie: heavy buttressed Victorian Gothic, the buttresses carried up the frontage terminating as pinnacles between the gabled dormers. **Tollemache House**, 1963, Sinclair Macdonald & Son, large rectangular block with bold, almost garish, mural by Caziel (Cazimir Zielemkiewicz). Though interesting as an example of 1960s design, Tollemache House sits uneasily in the traditional High Street. **Museum** (former library), 1910, Sinclair Macdonald, fills the corner with Wilson Street. Austere and dignified, the façade is enhanced by spare classical detailing. Amongst other items of local interest the museum houses the **herbarium** assembled by a local baker, Robert Dick, 1811-66, a skilled geologist and botanist, whose house at **8 Wilson Street**, is close by. *Museum open during summer months*
    High Street leads to Market Street, site of early burgh markets, to **Shore Street**, The Esplanade and Old St Peter's Kirk.

Tollemache House

Beaton

Robert Dick, 1811-66, was a baker in Thurso. He became an expert geologist and botanist. He loved the countryside and wide open spaces with their plants, once walking from Thurso to climb Morvern and back, a distance of 60 miles covered within 24 hours. *Sixty miles is a good walk to look at a hill. Oh those plants, those weary plants.* Samuel Smiles, 1878

Beaton

Shore Street; in foreground no.16/18. This and neighbouring houses have been modernised while those in the background, c.1955-60, harmonise in scale and use of local building materials

Shore Street separated from The Esplanade and sea by local authority **housing**. Many of these date from the 17th and 18th centuries, their original features almost unrecognisable 26 owing to upgrading. **16/18 Shore Street**, dated 1686 with initials DWKR, incorporates a two-storey rotund external stair tower of a former merchant's house.

Kippering-house

Beaton

The traditional kippered-herring trade, as widely practised … in Caithness ports, during the 19th century, has now all but ceased, like the herring-fishing itself … At its peak, however, during the middle decades of the century, the tall kipper-kilns of stone or timber, with their steeply pitched roofs and ridge ventilators, were familiar features … The principal buildings included facilities for preparing the fish (the fish-house or splitting-shed) usually with a loft above for packing the kippers and making up boxes, one or more kilns communicating directly with the fish-house, and desirably a yard for storage and a cart.
G D Hay & G P Stell, *Monuments of Industry*, 1986, p.26

Kippering-house, Shore Street, mid/late 19th century
One of the best, now rare survivals, of once flourishing industry associated with the herring fishing. The complex comprises kiln with long ridge louvres fitted with racks on which to hang the fish, fish-house with processing facilities and yard.

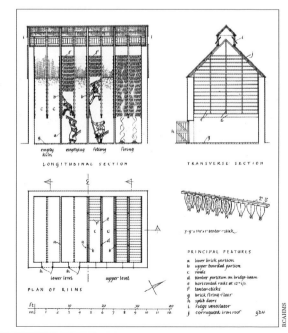

RCAHMS

Diagram of kippering kiln

Salvation Army Temple (former Independent (Secession) Chapel), Shore Street/Esplanade, *c.*1799

Large, plain and rectangular, following the conventional pattern of its time. Two round-arched windows light the south wall flanked by doorways (one now a window) with gallery windows at the upper stage. The building has had a chequered history, becoming a Congregational Chapel, then a store until finally purchased by Sir Tollemache Sinclair for the Salvation Army. **The Esplanade** was laid out as a coastal footpath in 1882.

Beaton

Above *Salvation Army Temple.* Left *Old St Peter's Church, illustration of 1829-32*

An Esplanade, 300 yards long, built in 1882, greatly improved the town, and may be said to be a monument to the public spirit and patriotism of the ladies of Thurso. A finely gravelled walk, eight feet wide, with neatly coped fence and turf border, has now been formed from the west ... along the cliffs ... where it joins the county road to Scrabster, a distance of fully 1¼ mile. The footway is undoubtedly one of the finest promenades in the north of Scotland, commanding, as it does, a magnificent view of sea and rock scenery.
J T Calder, *History of Caithness,* 1887, p.365

Thurso Museum

27 **Old St Peter's Church**, Wilson's Lane, from early 12th century

Roofless cruciform; medieval rectangular core, the chancel orientated eastwards in pre-Reformation manner but (unusually) curved internally and square ended externally. The chancel is low, accommodating a chamber above, reached by a wheel stair within the tower. The original medieval use of this chamber is obscure; after the Reformation it became the Session House. Equally obscure is the oblique angle of the tower, projecting between the east and south aisles (colour page 70).

After the Reformation (1560) Old St Peter's became the Presbyterian parish church, the internal layout altered to accommodate reformed worship and enlarged by the addition of the north aisle. The south aisle probably followed in early 17th century (during a period of Episcopal ministry) together with the enlarged north and west gable windows. This expansion doubled the size of the church and created a cruciform plan. The finest window

The tower of Old St Peter's abuts the church diagonally: one explanation that *could cause a tower to be built at an eccentric angle ... is the need for a marker for ships entering the Thurso River. It may be to this that the rocks of Kirk Ebb owe their name, rather than to the fanciful legend of the 'Kirk at the Ebb'.*
H Gordon Slade & George Watson

fills the south aisle gable; this is of five lights, the upper part with intricate interlacing Y-tracery below which there is further subdivision by three transoms (horizontal members). This window is similar to the great west window in Dornoch Cathedral, restored in 1835-7 (see *Sutherland* in this series).

Old St Peter's stands in a tightly packed **burial ground** enclosed by a high rubble wall with access from the street. The church was superseded as the parish church in 1832 by St Peter's and St Andrew's, Princes Street. *Guardianship Monument; open daily during summer*

Plan, Old St Peter's Church

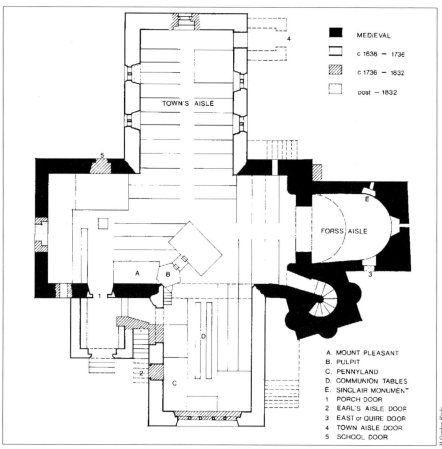

MEDiEVAL

c 1636 — 1736

c 1736 — 1832

post — 1832

TOWN'S AISLE

FORSS AISLE

A. MOUNT PLEASANT
B. PULPIT
C. PENNYLAND
D. COMMUNION TABLES
E. SINCLAIR MONUMEN⊤
1 PORCH DOOR
2 EARL'S AISLE DOOR
3 EAST or QUIRE DOOR
4 TOWN AISLE DOOR
5 SCHOOL DOOR

H Gordon Slade

The White House, Riverside Road, core from late 17th century; much restored *c.*1980
Regular four-bay frontage overlooks the river; it abuts Old St Peter's at the rear. The house was the property and home of the Revd William Innes, minister of Thurso, 1696-1737, who sold it

in 1734 (colour page 70). Many Highland ministers made their own housing arrangements until the late 18th/early 19th century when the provision of a manse became customary.

Miller Terrace

Between Riverside Road and Shore Street there is some sympathetic and interesting public housing. **Miller Terrace**, 1958, Sinclair Macdonald & Son, steps neatly down the slope while **Kirk View** flanks a pedestrian path leading to Old St Peter's. **Harbour Court**, 1985, Michael Lunny (Caithness District Council), is an attractive low-key group. **Morton Court**, Braehead, 1988, also Michael Lunny, is a small housing scheme exploiting Caithness stone and slate overlooking the harbour mouth. Houses in **Millers Lane** and **Riverside Road** have survived intact with sash-and-case glazing, but unsympathetic window replacement has taken its toll elsewhere.

28 **Meadow Well**, Mansons Lane, 1823
Small, circular wellhouse with conical stone roof. Though erected in 1818, it was not finished until five years later when the debt incurred in its construction was paid off. Also in Mansons Lane is the large crowstepped **Old**
29 **Brewery**, *c.*1798, established by a brewer named Alex Manson. The handsome building fronting the street as a three-storey elevation with brewer's house at one end was originally part of a courtyard complex incorporating ... *a Malt Barn, two Granaries ... an Iron Kiln of 24 feet in diameter ... Malt Deposit House, Tun Rooms, Still and Mash House.* The original roofing (probably local slate) has been replaced with corrugated iron, now a striking reddish hue. Exciting plans are still to be realised that this strong and positive building, a dominant contribution to urban Thurso, should become a creative glass centre (colour page 70).

Morton Court is named after octogenarian Councillor William Smith, a skilled footballer as a boy, nicknamed Morton after Scottish International Alan Morton, well-known contemporary of his youth.

Meadow Well

A brewery was envisaged in 1798 by Sir John Sinclair in order *to lessen the consumption of spirits, and supersede the importation of London porter, which has of late years been growing to an extensive height. The Statistical Account,* 1798. However, by 1839 a distillery had been introduced to the complex!

81

Plan, New Town of Thurso, c.1810

The New Town of Thurso was planned ... *according to the most regular plan that could be contrived and in a manner not only ornamental but also positively well adapted for preserving the health & promoting the convenience of the Inhabitants.*
Captain John Henderson, *General View of the Agriculture of the County of Caithness*, 1812

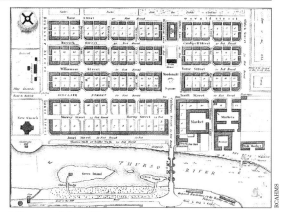

Thurso: New Town

The grid pattern new town of Thurso was constructed from *c*.1800 onward, centred on **Sir John's Square**, **St Peter's Church** and **Princes Street**, but abutting the old town with which it is fully integrated. The greater part is essentially domestic, the streets lined with single- and two-storey terraces and houses, the larger standing in their own gardens, homes for *all sorts and conditions of men* which was Sir John Sinclair's ideal. **Olrig Street**, **Traill Street** and Princes Street are the principal commercial thoroughfares.

Sir John's Square

Statue of Sir John Sinclair, 1856, by Sir Francis Chantrey. Sir John (who died in 1835) is portrayed dressed in the uniform of Colonel of the Rothesay and Caithness Fencibles, curiously combining trews with a sporran. The Fencibles were a force of 600 men raised by Sir John (see p.23). The square is aligned with the five-arched masonry **bridge** over the River Thurso constructed in 1887 to a design by Macbey & Gordon, engineers, to replace an early 19th-century bridge. Former **tollhouse** (correctly a

Thurso Bridge

pontage house for collection of *pontage* or bridge tolls; *pont* = bridge), *c.*1815; single storey with canted roadside frontage. Early bridge and tollhouse associated with Thomas Telford and development of road south by the Commission for Highland Roads & Bridges.

Sir George's Street
Episcopal Church, 1885, Alexander Ross;
30 chancel added 1905
Gothic and small, the entrance porch flanked by a slim belltower with conical roof. Simple interior: at rear hangs a fine panelled pew back with carved Munro eagle and dated 1676; part of the former family pew of the Revd Andrew Munro, of Coul, Ross-shire (see *Ross and Cromarty* in this series), Episcopal minister (Old St Peter's), Thurso, 1655-93. Opposite, former **cinema**, 1922, ?Sinclair Macdonald; chunky Modern Movement with oversize porthole windows. **Beaconsfield House**, late 19th century, Donald Leed. A substantial urban villa with canted bay windows set within its own garden.

Janet Street, 1800-10
An elegant terrace overlooking the River Thurso and meadows, of regular, two-storey, classical villas with rusticated quoins, emphasised central bay and each with slightly different detailing, linked by single-storey service buildings, some with pilastered frontages. Each house has a garden to the rear with stables and carriage house backing on to

Episcopal Church

Donald Leed, *c.*1844-1903, a builder in Glasgow who returned to his native Thurso, *c.*1880, to practise as an architect. He was Clerk of Works (local job architect) to Bank of Scotland, Thurso, 1896, and architect to Ulbster Estates for whom he *superintended various lodges and houses.*
Northern Ensign, 17 March 1903, and *Caithness Courier,* 13 March 1903

Left *Janet Street.* Below *Janet Street, c.1810*

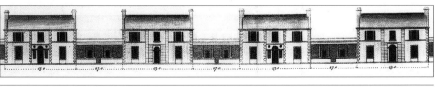

Sinclair Macdonald, 1859-1930, architect, was born in Brora where his father, Revd John Macdonald, was Free Church minister. Left an orphan, he was brought up by his Sinclair grandmother at Melvich, Sutherland. Educated in Aberdeen and Inverness he trained with Alexander Ross, Inverness, setting up practice in Thurso in 1889 (there was also a Wick office). He carried out a wide range of commissions in Caithness, always competent and sensitive to location and style as was his son, Hugh Macdonald, 1903-79, who subsequently practised with his father. The firm continues in Thurso as Sinclair Macdonald & Son.

Brabster Street. Sir John Sinclair lived in Charlotte Square when in Edinburgh – Janet Street is Thurso's happy response to the capital city's finest square.

Miller Primary School (former Miller Academy), 1934, Hugh Macdonald, Sinclair Macdonald & Son
Austerely dignified neo-Georgian, with long regular south front overlooking Janet Street and River Thurso.

Janet Street extends along the banks of the River Thurso. Several large late-Victorian gabled villas overlook the river, notably **Camfield House**, 1891, Sinclair Macdonald, and **Rosebank**, of similar vintage and style, undoubtedly by the same architect.

St Peter's and St Andrew's Church

William Burn, 1789-1870, son of Robert Burn, Edinburgh mason and architect. Trained with Robert Smirke, London. Established Edinburgh from 1814, developing a large practice in Scotland, mainly public buildings and country houses. In 1841 joined as partner by his former pupil and assistant, David Bryce (see p.55), who was in charge in Edinburgh from 1844 when Burn opened an office in London to look after his numerous English commissions. His ecclesiastical work was competent Gothic revival, the country houses ranging through Jacobean, Elizabethan to full-blown Scottish Baronial.

31 **Princes Street**
St Peter's and St Andrew's Church, 1832, William Burn
Stands at the junction of Princes Street and Sir John's Square as centrepiece of the new town and to replace Old St Peter's (see p.79). The substantial Gothic building is fronted by a three-stage tower with entrance in the base and buttressed flanks, the buttresses rising above the wallhead as pinnacles. Impressive galleried interior.

Princes Street is mainly lined with plain two-storey buildings, many marred by uncongenial shop fronts. **No 67** Princes Street, 1888, is a pretty single-storey villa at west end, the shaped entrance gable terminated with thistle finial while **Nos 71/73** are a delightful asymmetrical pair in similar gabled style.
32 **Greenacres**, *c.*1800, stands back from the street on a rise, the site of Ormlie Castle, and

Greenacres

has served as both Free and Church of
Scotland manses. The tall, two-storey-and-attic
house is a traditional Caithness dwelling with
wallhead gablet (see p.4): it is possible that the
building might incorporate earlier work.
Princes Street terminates with the gabled
Railway Station, 1874, Murdoch Paterson;
also standard Highland Railway wooden **goods
shed**; the former **engine shed** now serves as a
carpet shop near the extreme end of Janet
Street. In 1984 the station reception area was
sympathetically refurbished by Lyndall Leet
with considerable use of local flagstone.

Ormlie Road
Old Ormlie Farm, 18th century
Symmetrical farmhouse with central wallhead
gablet, later additions and steading. Though
depressingly abandoned in the middle of a
housing estate, the dignity of the house is
evident in its traditional proportions, local
masonry and a few slender glazing bars in the
sash windows.

Thurso High School

Thurso College (former Technical College)
and **Thurso High School**
Neighbours on a greenfield site. Thurso
College, from mid-1950s, a rectangular glazed
slab on stilts constructed in progressive stages,
the current tinted glazing installed 1996. High
School composed of a series of integrated
blocks, the original building designed by
Sir Basil Spence in 1958, coinciding with the
establishment of Dounreay atomic power
station which brought an increase in
population and consequent demand for more
school accommodation.

Dunbar Hospital

Dunbar Hospital, from 1882
Baronial, the entrance decorated with cable
moulding recalling Ackergill Tower and the
work of David Bryce. Later flanking pavilions
linked with the centre block. The hospital was
donated by Mr Dunbar of Scrabster and the
foundation stone laid by HRH The Duke of
Edinburgh, 21 January 1882. Originally

intended for the *relief of suffering from disease of any kind and for support of a limited number of aged persons who have seen better days* who were accommodated in the main building and two cottage dwellings. From 1924 it has served Thurso as a hospital for the sick, the infirm elderly accommodated elsewhere.

Ormlie Hill Dental Centre (former waterworks), *c*.1880, converted 1994, The Leet Rodgers Practice
Unassuming single-storey stone building given a new working life with well-lit interior and cheerful wood-lined reception area.

Public Library

Beaton

THE MILLER INSTITUTION *Was Opened on the 1st day of April and put under the direction of Two Teachers, both capable and respectable, determined to Teach effectively, at the following rates per Quarter:*
For English Reading and Arithmetic ... 3s.0d.
For all the above, with Grammar and Geography ... 4s.0d.
For all the above, with History, Writing, and Arithmetic to its full extent, including Book-keeping ... 5s.0d.
Advertisement, Thurso, 1 April 1862

33 **Davidson's Lane**
Public Library (originally Miller Institution), 1859-62
Handsome, classical, single-storey former academy axially facing Sinclair Street and visible from Olrig Street and the junction with the old town. It is fronted by a pedimented portico behind which rises a slender two-stage circular domed clock tower. The school was ... *erected by Mr Miller for the town of Thurso ... according to plans prepared by Mr Scott, architect, Edinburgh. The expense will be from £1200 to £1500 (John o'Groat Journal,* 15 December 1859). The donor, the Revd Alexander Miller, was a native of Thurso and Free Church minister of Buckie, Banffshire. The dome was an afterthought, as a further £200 had to be raised for ... *such a thing will undoubtedly add greatly to the appearance of our town as well as to that of the handsome building on which it is to be placed (John o'Groat Journal,* 15 November 1860). Hanging in the library is a fine *credible and correct* topographical print by John Warner Scott, artist and architect of the building, about whom virtually nothing is known (colour page 70). **Riverbank Medical Centre**, also

Riverbank Medical Centre

Beaton

Davidson's Lane, 1994, Roxby Park & Baird. Tall, canted glazed frontage flooding light into reception area; south elevation fronts Janet Street in domestic scale with local rubble cladding and perky oriel windows.

Sinclair Street is visually terminated by the Public Library (see Davidson's Lane): this axial point is in contrast to the domestic nature of the street, largely fronted by plain houses opening directly to the pavement. The exception is the **West Church** (former Free Church), 1859-60, David Smith: Gothic with tall spire punctuating the skyline. Former **post office**, 1916, Sinclair Macdonald, fills the corner with Sir George's Street. Gabled, well-mannered, domestic in character and faintly Arts & Crafts.

Beaton

Above Former post office. Left 25-35 Traill Street; handsome terrace of shops with domestic accommodation above

Beaton

David Smith, 1814-79, architect, Thurso, one of *Thurso's oldest and respected townsmen*, was at his drawing board 24 hours before his death. His tombstone in the New Cemetery, Thurso, bears a marble likeness of this bearded, be-whiskered gentleman.
Caithness Courier, 7 August 1879

Traill Street
Nos 25-35, 1878-9, David Smith; handsome two-storey terrace of shops with original shop windows and chunky detailing including dog-tooth moulding at the wallhead. The terrace expresses in architectural terms the confidence of the retailers trading from the premises in Thurso's busiest commercial street. **No 33/35** has a grand staircase with turned balusters and an upstairs room with plaster ceiling decorated with Prince of Wales' feathers, commemorating the Prince and Princess of Wales' visit to Thurso in 1876. **No 37** continues in the same vein with another dignified shop front. **Clydesdale Bank** (former Aberdeen Town and County Bank), 1866, J Russell Mackenzie, turns the corner of Cowie Lane with bowed angle and solid conviction.

Clydesdale Bank (former Aberdeen Town and County Bank); note separate entrances to banking hall and to manager's accommodation at first floor

RCAHMS

Bank of Scotland, Olrig Street

Beaton

Olrig Street

34 **Bank of Scotland** (former British Linen Bank), 1897, J M Dick Peddie
Imposing, symmetrical polished sandstone frontage, mullioned and transomed windows and tall, shaped and finialled centre Flemish gable. Next is the grandiose former **St Andrew's Free Church**, 1870, J Russell Mackenzie. St Andrew's has a tall spire, large traceried Gothic windows in the crowstepped and gabled street frontage and flanking gallery stair bay with faceted roof. The church is no longer in use and the soaring interior stripped of many fittings. It remains an impressive landmark, particularly from Rose Street.

Police Station, *c.*1970, Jenkins & Marr Slate-hung and functional but out of character
35 with its immediate neighbours. **Masonic Hall**, 1873, David Smith, is a handsome former volunteer drill hall, castellated and suitably military with angle bartizans and crenellated central tower housing a porch at base. The hall is fronted by cast-iron spearhead railings mounted on low wall with grandiose crenellated gatepiers and cast-iron entrance gates.

Below Campbell Street. Bottom 21-25 Rose Street

Beaton

Campbell Street, 1820-30
The compact streetscape is enhanced by the alternate advancing and recessing of small two-storey, three-window houses, giving an added interest to otherwise plain frontages.

Rose Street and **George Street** have some charming single-storey villas dating from mid- and later 19th century fronted by small gardens. In Rose Street, **Nos 21-25** are of interest, each house with gabled and pilastered

Beaton

entrance bay, the principal room lit by a larger three-light window. **Nos 9 & 11** Rose Street are pedimented. **Nos 2-7** George Street, 1877, consist of three paired two-bay cottages, with crenellated canted bay windows, canted dormers and ornamented or dated skewputts: these are also fronted by small gardens. Here **No 4** has an inscribed door lintel reading *This house was visited by HRH THE DUKE OF EDINBURGH 21ST JANUARY 1882, on the occasion of his laying the foundation stone of the Dunbar Hospital.* **No 7** was the home of Donald Leed, architect (see p.83).

9 & 11 Rose Street; domesticity with dignity

Granville Street and Pennyland

Pentland House (former Church of Scotland manse), Granville Street, 1770
Pilastered doorway and wallhead gablet dignify the regular, plain front and central gablet: broad Caithness-type, gable-end chimneystacks: rear wing added in 1831 (colour p.71). **Pennyland Farm**, *c*.1790, a substantial whitewashed farmhouse, is in similar Caithness tradition with regular frontage. Adjoining farm **steading** linked to house by crenellated and turreted screen wall. This was the birthplace (1845) of Sir William Smith, founder of the Boys' Brigade.

Sir William Smith, WS, 1854-1914, was born at Pennyland, moving to Glasgow after his father's death in 1869. There he played an active part in church affairs. Seeing that older boys found Sunday School tedious, he established the Boys' Brigade to offer a lively programme, including games and camping, within a corps devoted to the *Advancement of Christ's Kingdom among Boys and promotion of habits of Obedience, Reverence, Discipline, Self-Respect and all that tends towards a true Christian manliness.*

St Anne's Roman Catholic Church,
Sweyn Road, 1960, Hugh Macdonald of Sinclair Macdonald & Son
Simple gabled structure clad in dark stained vertical weatherboarding with single-storey Caithness rubble porch. The groined interior, a modern interpretation of cruck-frame support, is flooded with light from the glazed west gable, further enhanced by the pale wooden furnishings. A fine carved relief of St Anne, Virgin Mary and Holy Child hangs in chancel. Ecclesiastical Sixties architecture at its best, dignified modernity at ease with tradition.

Left Interior, St Anne's Roman Catholic Church, flooded with light from glazed west gable. Below St Anne's Roman Catholic Church

Timber-clad housing, Sweyn Road

Sweyn and **Castlegreen Roads** and area
Lined with pleasantly domestic timber-clad
houses dating from the 1950s, constructed in
pairs, each with small single-storey gable wing,
multi-pane glazing and some with dormers
breaking the wallhead. These homes line
gently winding streets creating a welcoming,
homely environment in marked contrast to the
gaunt, three-storey, *c*.1960 blocks of flats at
angle of Sweyn Road and Castlegreen Road.

Thurso: East
Local authority residential development,
expanding the town across the Thurso River in
the 1960s and 1970s. **Queen's Square** and
Queen's Terrace, **Castletown Road** are
enhanced with Caithness stone cladding and rich
brown local roof slates, in marked contrast to the
flatted blocks flanking the A9 near Millbank,
incongruous despite remodelling, 1995-6.

Thurso Castle, 1872-8, David Smith
Largely demolished in 1952 leaving a roofless
silhouette to dominate the skyline east of the
town, the skeletal ghost of the grandiose
castellated mansion built by Sir Tollemache
Sinclair. Its spiky Gothic grandeur is
replicated in the contemporary arched

*Below Thurso Castle, c.1660,
superseded 1872. Illustration from
Jones'* Views of Scotch Seats, *c.1830.
Bottom Gatelodge and entrance arch
to Thurso Castle. Right Thurso
Castle, castellated grandeur, now a
fire-gutted shell*

gateway and **gatelodge**, presumably also the work of David Smith.

Millbank
Long, *c*.1800 former flaxmill later adapted as an engineering works and foundry. The associated two-storey range includes the 36 former **Thurso Mill**, now a youth centre. Unusual, tall, stepped west gable enhances the mill in the landscape when viewed from the riverside walks and Janet Street.

Left Thurso Mill. Below Harold's Tower, engraving of c.1790

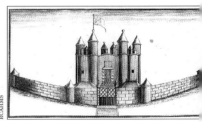

37 **Harold's Tower**, 1780-90
This romantic folly – a landmark on the eastern skyline of the town – was erected by Sir John Sinclair of Ulbster to commemorate the Norse Earl Harold, killed in the Battle of Clairdon in 1195 and buried hereabouts in the field still called Chapel Field. The chunky hexagonal mausoleum has angles punctuated by crude pencil turrets and an inscribed plaque bearing the legend *This is the burial place of the Sinclairs of Ulbster*. The mausoleum superseded the family vault at Ulbster (see p.23).

EARL HAROLD the Younger to the Laird of Ulbster: *Know, Sir, that I was slain in battle, about the year 1190, near your park ... and buried within that piece of ground, and had an elegant chapel erected over my grave, the stones whereof are built now in your inclosure* (drystone walls) *in that place ... I lost my life in battle, endeavouring to recover my property out of the hands of a wicked and daring tyrant, Earl Harold the Elder ... Be pleased to inclose my grave in a decent manner, so as not to become the resting-place of animals, or that my bones be not ploughed up ... it will yield you the most manly and sensible pleasure ... which will perpetuate your memory to posterity.*
Revd Alexander Pope to Sir John Sinclair of Ulbster, on behalf of Earl Harold, *The Statistical Account*, 1798

Harold's Tower

SCRABSTER
Small 19th-century village tucked under the cliffside: fronted by large **harbour** constructed from *c*.1850, now overwhelmed by late 20th-century expansion. From here the ferries come and go for Orkney, Shetland and the Faroe Islands; besides passengers and vehicles they transport cattle, for which there are harbourside pens from whence the mooing of reluctant kine competes with the persistent calling of gulls! Early 19th-century **icehouse** built into cliff face indicates former commercial salmon fishing. **Lifeboat House**, 1957 (replacing lifeboat house of 1906 destroyed by fire in 1956); tall shed fronted by long concrete **slipway** giving immediate access to deep water at all tides. Contemporary lifeboats, however, are now moored in harbour and urgent, dramatic slipway launches are rare.

Scrabster House

Scrabster House, dated 1834
Stands on a mound commanding Scrabster and Thurso Bay, probably a long-established site. Earlier house dated 1834 buried within the sparkling white mansion, baronialised in style of David Bryce (see p.55).

Scrabster Harbour Trust Headquarters

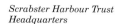

Scrabster Harbour Trust Headquarters, 1989, The Leet Rodgers Practice
Two-storey, regularly fronted building with recessed entrance framed with dressed stone below simple wallhead gablet. Regular windows provide generous internal light, enhanced with pale wooden fittings and furnishings. Architecturally a good neighbour to the mixed buildings of the Scrabster harbour front, but mirroring the authority and administration housed within.

[38] **Holborn Head Lighthouse**, 1862,
D & T Stevenson
The white-painted walled lighthouse complex
stands out against the green slope of Holborn
Head, commanding Thurso Bay and the
Pentland Firth. The short circular tower is
mounted on a two-storey, double-pile building
combining both keepers' and lighthouse-
servicing accommodation.

Holbornhead, *c.*1700, restored and
modernised 1993, The Leet Rodgers Practice
Interesting and very unusual two-storey
crowstepped laird's house on cliff edge
overlooking Thurso Bay. Regular three-window
west-facing elevation with long and short
rubble dressings framing windows (see also
Hempriggs House, p.25).

Holbornhead

BRIMS AND FORSS
Brims Castle, 16th century
Square, homely, three-storey, L-plan fortalice
with adjoining crowstepped two-storey house of
*c.*1800. Rear stair tower, with blocked original
first-floor entrance and small open angle
bartizan with elaborate chequered corbelling
(see also Keiss, p.55). The tower house is
enclosed by a walled court entered through a
tall round-headed arched entrance with worn
moulded jambs. Brims Castle stands above the
Port of Brims, a tiny inlet which formerly
served as a boat haven on this inhospitable
stretch of rocky coast. The layout of tower
house and arched entrance (the latter may not
be in its original 16th-century position) are
similar to Carrick House, Eday, 1633 (see
Orkney in this series). The castle and dwelling,
originally belonging to the Sinclair family, are
abandoned; they stand neglected within an
active farm complex and surrounded by large
fields. These fields, and the approach road, are

Top *Slab fence, Brims.* Above
*Drystone dykes at Brims with raised
slabs carrying wire as additional
sheep deterrent.* Left *Brims Castle,
later farmhouse at right*

St Mary's Chapel

notable for superb slab fences and drystone dykes; some of the latter have intermediate stone posts carrying a wire to heighten the dyke as an additional deterrent for sheep.

39 **St Mary's Chapel**, Crosskirk, probably 12th century
One of the oldest ecclesiastical buildings in Caithness. The chapel stands in walled burial ground on a headland overlooking Crosskirk Bay. Though roofless, the rubble walls of the rectangular nave and small square-ended chancel (probably later rebuild on early foundation) are almost complete. The entrance in the long south wall is modern; those in the west and east (latter to chancel) walls with flat lintel and inclined jambs are original.
Guardianship Monument, open at all times. Access by field path only (¾ mile)

Forss House Hotel, c.1800
Substantial and unusual M-gabled, double-pile house overlooking the Forss Water. Symmetrical five-bay south front with large ground-floor windows, dominant tall chimneystacks and later rear crenellated entrance wing (1939). The naturally defensive site enclosed on three sides by the river suggests it was occupied before the mansion.

Right *Forss House Hotel.*
Below *Forss Mill*

Bridge of Forss, early 19th century
Two-arch masonry bridge spanning the Forss Water. This bridge superseded the mid-18th-century humpback bridge a mile or so upstream (ND 041675). **Forss Mills**, early 19th century, one on each side of the river. The larger, on the east bank, has a piended local slate roof, overshot wheel and gabled dwellinghouse set back at south gable. Set against a backdrop of trees and fields, these buildings form a picturesque group beside the fast-flowing river (colour page 71).

Beaton

Dounreay Nuclear Power Development Establishment

Dounreay was the site of the original castle of the Mackay family, Lords of Reay, later of Tongue (see *Sutherland* in this series). Its 20th-century role is that of the Dounreay Nuclear Power Development Establishment which came into being in the early 1950s, in operation by 1959 and the first in the world to supply electricity commercially in 1962. The Prototype Fast Reactor (PFR) began operating in 1974 with the dual role of providing power to the national grid and research and development facilities. The now-familiar sphere and the large rectangular buildings that make up the Dounreay atomic complex have brought a substantial late 20th-century architectural and technological presence to Caithness.

Dounreay Nuclear Power Development Establishment, from 1950

Occupying the site of late 16th-century Dounreay Castle, former seat of the Lords of Reay (see *Sutherland* in this series). Small, three-storey, L-plan tower house, now roofless. Construction of the familiar and splendidly massed spherical Dounreay Fast Reactor started in 1955, becoming operational in 1959. A continuous construction programme during the 1960s and 1970s created a complex of industrially related buildings. *Exhibition devoted to the Establishment is sited in the airfield control tower and usually open to the public during the summer months* (colour page 72).

REAY VILLAGE

Small, attractive village, with traditional housing surrounding central green. The stumpy market cross standing on a grassy verge is said to have been rescued from the site of Old Reay which was submerged by the sea at an unknown date.

Reay Parish Church, 1739

Plain, white-harled, T-plan church with distinctive tower at east gable, it is a familiar landmark on the eastern outskirts of Reay. Regular frontage to roadside revealing blocked doors and windows, with forestair at rear serving tower. The large Y-tracery window was inserted in the west gable in 1933 when the seating was also renewed. Beside the doorway is an anchor point for the *jougs,* iron fetters to restrain wrongdoers as a public punishment. Traditional internal layout includes a long central communion table and imposing 18th-century pulpit, complete with pilastered backboard and hexagonal sounding-board, standing against the south wall. Sandside gallery with panelled frontage fills north aisle (colour page 72). The church was built during the incumbency of the Revd Alexander Pope, minister 1734-79, a man of letters who

Below *Reay Village.* Bottom *Reay Parish Church, with tower as a landmark for seamen*

Beaton

Beaton

In 1751 a waterspout *laid bare the foundations of a town on the west side of the burn of Reay between the village called Old Reay and the sea. The old village had a market cross, now removed to New Reay, a village built to the westward of the former. Origines Parochiales Scotae, vol ii, part 2, 1855*

contributed an appendix on northern Scotland to Thomas Pennant's *A Tour of Scotland in 1769*. Alexander Pope rode his pony to London and back in order to meet his namesake, the poet!

Old Burial Ground

Probably medieval, site of parish church until 1739. Walled burial ground, with fine stone slab pedestrian steps built into dyke. Burial mausoleum of Mackays of Bighouse (see *Sutherland* in this series) was originally part of the demolished church. Family mural memorials include that to Lt-Col George Mackay, died 1798; the grey and white marble plaque is flanked by mourning riflemen.

SANDSIDE

Sandside Harbour, *c*.1830, James Bremner

An attractive harbour built by Major William Innes of Sandside for both trade and fishing. It is sheltered at the west by high ground and looks east over the Pentland Firth and Dounreay. The stonework is varied and excellent, the seaward faces of the harbour walls of vertically laid masonry. Some *c*.1830 **cottages** and a fine three-storey **fishing store** line the quayside.

A very neat and commodious harbour has lately been built in the bay of Sandside by Major Innes, on which upwards of £3,000 have already been expended while it encourages and promotes trade and commerce, it is also of great advantage to the herrying-fishing. New Statistical Account, xv, 1840, p.20

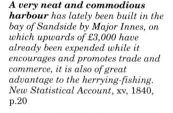

Above *Sandside Harbour, fishing store and net-drying poles*. Right *Sandside Harbour*

Sandside House, from 1751; additions, 1889, James Matthews

Large rambling mansion on a site of considerable antiquity and importance. The original portion a typical Caithness laird's house of 1751 with a regular five-window frontage, pretty shaped centre gablet and late 19th-century ground-floor bay windows. This frontage faced east over the Pentland Firth, enabling residents to note the coming and going of shipping. Some enlargement in 1840, but its present south entrance front dates from 1889, making bold use of mullioned and transomed windows, flanked each side by

Left *Sandside House and walled garden.* Above *Sandside House, 1751 laird's house (later ground-floor bay windows)*

crowstepped wings. In 1889 the mansion was connected with the road (by then superseding the sea as the main artery of communication) by a driveway with gatelodge.

Early settlement at Sandside is commemorated by various incised **Pictish stones**: there was an earlier house (or houses) on the site, indicated by both Timothy Pont (Blaeu's *Atlas,* 1654, see frontispiece and p.64) and Roy's military survey, *c.*1747-55. Only a detailed survey of Sandside House would reveal whether portions of any of these are incorporated in the present fabric.

Sandside House is notable for a series of magnificent high **garden walls**, its 18th/19th-century two-seater **privy** in the garden and the early 19th-century **dovecote** housing birds for sport (rather than the table, see p.103). The birds (live forerunners of clay pigeons) were released from baskets for shooting practice to marksmen standing in the field nearby. The flight holes had no alighting ledges on the field side, for the birds were not intended to return home to the loft!

There is also a fine range of 18th-century **farm buildings**, in particular the rectangular, gable-ended **kiln-barn** of Banffshire type, rather than the circular traditional Caithness bottle-shaped kiln (see p.35), with canted stair tower leading to the kiln floor abutting the south gable. This is not surprising, for though the Inneses had long been resident in Caithness, the family originated from Banffshire and Moray. Sandside, sited amidst lime-rich green fields, belonged to the Inneses of that name until the late 19th century. The estate, with its handsome mansion, outstanding farm buildings, fine garden and harbour, is one of the most interesting and attractive in Caithness.

Below *Dovecote, Sandside House.* Bottom *Kiln-barn, Sandside House; note canted gable stair tower leading to kiln floor. Contemporary barn at right angles*

SHEBSTER, BROUBSTER AND SHURRERY

Sparsely populated area with scattered lochs and bounded by hills on the west.

Reay Free Church

Reay Free Church, Achimenach, Shebster, 1844

Grouped with former **manse** and **school**; double-fronted, double-aisled plan peculiar to Caithness, with hexagonal minister's porch projecting at the west. A confident architectural composition broadcasting the ability of the Free Kirk to break from the past and create its own architectural forms. Though now isolated and disused, the interior sadly gutted, the group reveals the strength of the Free Church movement besides the large local population, of which a considerable proportion were adherents: in *c.*1855 the attendance was 700 (see p.6).

Right and below *Cottages, Broubster Square*

Broubster and **Shurrery** are scattered settlements south of Shebster. **Broubster**
40 **Square**, 1839, an unusual hollow square of longhouse-type cottages (see Laidhay, p.16), now of U-plan formation as the cottages forming the west side, flanking the road, have disappeared. These cottages were built to house some of the tenants relocated from the Broubster and Shurrery estates, one still occupied in 1960. Each combines domestic

accommodation and byre/stable; in the centre of the north range (the most complete) there is a barn with threshing/winnowing floor, the draught for winnowing provided by opposing openings. Narrow strips of cultivated land were behind each row of cottages. Broubster Square is a curious combination of the formal estate layout of the hollow square enclosed by vernacular longhouses, suggesting that though the laird provided the land and probably dictated the site plan, the construction of the cottages was left to the residents who kept to the traditional form they knew and understood. The individual build of each cottage is verified by the slight variations in construction and plan form (colour page 72).

Recumbent cruck truss: in treeless Caithness the timber was often of poor quality and jointed

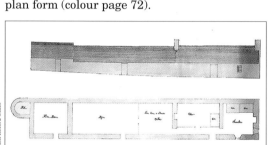

Plan of Alexander Macleods House and Premifses (sic) *in Latheron by Alexander Davidson L,S, 1835. A contemporary drawing of a longhouse similar to those at Broubster. This drawing indicates that the longhouse was by no means just a peasant home for Alexander Macleod could afford to commission a Land Surveyor to prepare the plan. From left to right, Kiln, Kiln Barn, Byre, Fire room, Cellar (Room), Chamber (Parlour). Both Cellar and Chamber have box beds; the Chamber is the only room with a window. Note that the Fire room has a central hearth and direct access to the byre (see pp. 7, 8, 16).*

A mile north are a scatter of pre-clearance **farmsteads** with grain kilns and internal nooks for geese (as in Orkney). Downhill from the settlement are the twin **canals**, an over-ambitious attempt to divert the Forss Water and drain the marshy Leans of Broubster.

[41] **Shurrery Chapel-of-Ease**, 1838
Simple T-plan (disused) church with four regular windows in long south front fitted with shutters (still in place); a ball finial at each gable is the only decoration; small rear vestry. The church was built to serve a large and scattered population (which has now dwindled away), too far from Reay Parish Church for regular worship. The interior is now gutted and a large entrance slapped in the east gable. Shurrery became a *Quoad Sacra* parish in its own right in 1902. There is a gabled former **manse**, also 1838, close by, which together with the church, were financed by William Innes of Sandside (see p.96) and endowed in 1902 by Mr Pilkington (subsequent owner of Sandside) in memory of his son killed in the South African War, 1901.

Below and bottom Shurrery Chapel-of-Ease. Plain building constructed to serve an isolated community

St Drostan (Trostan, died *c*.610) was a member of the royal Irish Cosgrach family: he became a monk under St Columba and first Abbot of Deer Monastery, Aberdeenshire, after which he went to live as a hermit in Glenesk. There are five dedications to this saint in Caithness. Close to the Westfield burial ground is a small rise called Priest Hillock, place-name evidence to the pre-Reformation nature of the chapel site.

Top *St Drostan's burial ground.*
Above *Medieval hog-back type tombstones.* Right *Westfield House*

Hog-back tombs, shaped as their name implies and tegulated (carved with dummy roofing shingles), are Norse. The smooth, almost cigar-like examples at St Drostan's are probably a medieval survival of this earlier tradition.

Westfield Bridge

WESTFIELD

Westfield House, mid-18th century Elegant, double-pile, M-gabled house with regular five-window frontage and nicely moulded eaves cornice: the slightly longer first-floor windows indicate the original principal floor (see p.5). A large range of outbuildings of varying date are sited at right angles between house and lane. Behind the house, a small, square, early 19th-century, two-storey **dovecote** with pigeon accommodation in the upper storey only. Westfield, with neighbouring St Drostan's, is a site of some antiquity, the present house a successor to others.

St Drostan's **burial ground**, site of earlier chapel dedicated to St Drostan. This is a peaceful place sheltered by trees with a stream flowing close by. A pair of simple hog-back-type gravestones, probably early medieval, indicate the great age of the site. **Westfield Bridge**, early 19th century, spans the River Thurso with two unequal masonry arches split by triangular buttresses/cutwaters.

HALKIRK

Halkirk overlooks the wide but shallow valley of the River Thurso stretching from Thurso Bay to Loch Watten, an area of fertile farmland. Halkirk was the ecclesiastical centre of the Bishopric of Caithness and Sutherland before Bishop Gilbert Murray moved the see to Dornoch in 1224 (see *Sutherland* in this

Halkirk

series). The place name is probably old Norse *Ha-kirk-ja* meaning High Church, indicating the ecclesiastical connection. The village is now essentially 19th and 20th century, laid out on a grid plan devised by Sir John Sinclair of Ulbster in 1803; though the plan is evident, the original village was never completed and some plots not built on until the 1980s.

Braal Castle, 12th/13th century
Ruinous Braal Castle was originally the principal seat of the Earls of Caithness. It is beautifully situated amongst trees on banks of the River Thurso: square, two-storey, drystone masonry tower somewhat similar to Old Wick (see p.25). It has been succeeded in name by a 19th-century regularly fronted, castellated house with angle bartizans, now divided as flats.

Old Parish Church, 1753
T-plan church (disused), the long south wall lit by two large and two smaller arched windows. Though stripped of its internal fittings, the sloping floor indicates that the seating was raked, a feature of some Caithness parish churches. The church is surrounded by a tightly packed burial ground on the outskirts of the village.

Halkirk was the ecclesiastical centre of the Bishopric of Caithness and Sutherland before Bishop Gilbert Murray moved the see to Dornoch, Sutherland, in 1224 (see *Sutherland* in this series). The ruinous 12th/13th-century **Braal Castle** was the principal seat of the Earls of Caithness passing to the Sinclairs of Ulbster.

Left *Old Parish Church.*
Below *Church of Scotland*

Church of Scotland (former Free Church), 1886, Alexander Ross
Chunky Romanesque with campanile and large rose window in entrance gable. Unusual architectural style for Alexander Ross, who mostly favoured the Gothic for ecclesiastical use. This building replaced the double-gabled, typical mid-19th-century Caithness-type **Free Church** of 1844, in the centre of the village, subsequently converted as cottage dwellings. (For Alexander Ross see p.36.)

Ross Institute, 1912, Sinclair Macdonald
Handsome baronial village hall dominating its
corner site overlooking the River Thurso; three-
stage clock tower with porch in the base.
Ulbster Arms, dated 1878, style of Donald
Leed; large canted bay windows flank the main
entrance, the magpie-painted façade decorated
with cable and dog-tooth moulding (see also
25-35 Traill Street, Thurso). **War Memorial**,
D & A Davidson, a white marble representation
of a war widow with child on pedestal, she with
a fringed plaid over her head and the small boy
in Highland dress.

*Above Ross Institute. Right Ulbster
Arms*

The Ross Institute was gifted to
Halkirk by Mr John Ross, a native
of the village who emigrated to New
Zealand. He stipulated that there
should be no *Travelling Theatrical
Companies and no intoxicating
drink* allowed on the premises. The
clock, the first electric clock fitted
in any public building in Scotland,
was donated by David Murray, also
of Halkirk.

Fairview, 1854-6
Former Thurso (and all parishes except Wick
and Latheron) Combination Poorhouse; the
parishes combining to accommodate their poor
and needy. Long, austere, two-storey, 18-bay
gabled frontage. Sited on the outskirts of the
village, it was constructed to accommodate the
destitute and needy whose care was shared in
combination. The building was converted into
local authority flats in the early 1980s.

Fairview

AIMSTER AND SKINNET
Both sited north of Halkirk on the B874.

Old Aimster Farmhouse, mid-18th century
Caithness laird's house with symmetrical
frontage and shaped wallhead gable (*nepus*
gable). Also an unusual block of flatted
farmworkers' dwellings of *c*.1870.

Old Skinnet House, late 18th century
Charming and unusual essay in naïve rural
classicism, the shallow, pedimented, two-storey
frontage matched by similar pedimented
pavilion wings and a long rear catslide roof.
Sadly the house has been abandoned (colour
page 71). **St Thomas**, Skinnet, is the site of a
pre-Reformation chapel.

SPITTAL AND WESTERDALE
Spittal is a small township, with a working flagstone quarry. Site of the medieval *(ho)spital* offering shelter to pilgrims travelling to or from the great shrine of St Magnus, Orkney.

Westerdale, a wide area of undulating farmland well watered by the River Thurso, enclosed by distant hills marching across the western skyline. In summer the landscape is green against a blue backdrop of mountains and sky. The single-track road leads westwards to the moors with scattered lochs and isolated shooting lodges.

Left Dale House, mid-18th-century centre block flanked (r) by 1910 service wing and (l) by 1933 drawing-room wing. Below Apex flight hole and interior, Dale House beehive dovecote with drystone nesting boxes

42 **Dale House**, Westerdale, from mid-18th century
Handsome, white-painted, two- and three-storey mansion with east-facing entrance front; though of different builds the overall style of this linear house is homogeneous. Tall, three-storey, symmetrical, five-window original centre block with first-floor entry reached by later forestair. Flanking north range with long first-floor windows, incorporating service quarters. This wing existed by 1871 (1st edn Ordnance Survey); the 1910 datestone probably commemorates alterations or remodelling. The fine, south, two-storey drawing-room block was added in 1933 overlooking garden and wide panorama of fields, moors and mountains. **Dovecote**, 17th/early 18th-century, four-stage *beehive doocot* with doorway in east side, the stages effecting a gentle batter (inward slope; see p.4). Wide, circular apex entrance for birds lined with 350 nesting stone boxes. The dovecote stands beside the River Thurso, within a later circular **walled garden**.

Beehive dovecotes are rotund and domed, so called because they resemble old-fashioned straw beeskeps. The cotes rise in diminishing courses, the interior lined with stone nesting boxes, tiered to the circular apex flight hole. This is the earliest of many different types, lectern or lean-to with single-pitch roof, rectangular and circular. The lectern was favoured in Scotland in the 17th and 18th centuries, the model found in Scotland and the south of France but rarely in England. Doves (not wood pigeons) were farmed for their flesh, providing meat for pies and stews. The practice of rearing the birds declined from 1800 as farming methods changed. About a dozen cotes survive in Caithness.

103

Westerdale Mill on banks of River Thurso

Below *Westerdale Free Church.*
Bottom *Strathmore Lodge*

Westerdale Bridge, 1834, spans the tumbling Thurso River, an elegant twin-arched masonry structure. Disused **Westerdale Mill** on side of the water and farm on the other form an attractive group by the bridge.

Westerdale Free Church, 1844
Simple, little-altered T-plan kirk (disused) with shallow pointed-headed windows. Good canopied pulpit fronted by clerk's desk. Unusually, this building does not conform to the *c*.1844 double-fronted pattern of Caithness Free Churches (see p.6). There are isolated shooting lodges on the moors at **Strathmore**, **Dalwillan** and **Lochdhu**.

43 **Strathmore Lodge**, early and late 19th century, greatly remodelled *c*.1930, by Sinclair Macdonald
Shining white, rambling shooting lodge overlooking the River Thurso dominated by circular tower with corbelled, conical upper storey.

Strathmore burial ground, early 19th century
Small and square beside the River Thurso, enclosed by fine drystone wall which is a credit to the drystone dyker's craft. There is no gated entrance; access is by projecting slab steps corbelled from the outside wallface and a wide flight of stone steps inside, the intervening wallhead forming a broad platform on which to rest the coffin (colour page 72). The tombstone of Isabel Polson, who died 1 December 1842, bears (unusually in Caithness) a Gaelic inscription: Psalm CVII, v6. *Air chiumhne gu brath bithidh am firean* (And the righteous shall be had in everlasting remembrance) indicating the use of Gaelic in this distant inland strath, originally Strath Mhor (Gaelic = large) (see p.4).

Lochdhu Lodge, 1895, perhaps David Smith (died 1879) but executed by Donald Leed for Ulbster Estates
Verges on the exotic. The idiosyncratic architectural features of this lonely house include baronial detailing, a profusion of heavy cable moulding, four-storey glazed projecting octagonal stairwell and bi-coloured, zigzag patterned, slate roof.

Lochdhu Lodge, photographed c.1985

From Westerdale the B870 leads eastwards to the **Mybster Crossroads**, Spittal, continuing to the A882 (Thurso/Wick), from where **Sordale**, **Stemster** and **Watten** can be visited. Also south to Latheron (see p.17) over the bleak Causeymire.

CAUSEYMIRE
The *Causeway Mire*, a wide, damp and lonely area flanking the main A895 Spittal/Latheron road. A stone causeway was probably laid to facilitate travel, perhaps for the pilgrims making their way to and from the hospice at Spittal (see p.103). The track was clearly defined as *The myre calsey* by the cartographer Timothy Pont (see p.64) and is thought to have been repaired by Cromwell's troops, *c.*1650. It has been in use as a highway ever since.

Below Causeymire Church of Scotland. Bottom Plaque on Causeymire Church of Scotland

44 **Causeymire Church of Scotland**, 1842, later United Free (grid ref. ND 173483)
Isolated and very simple on the site of an earlier *mission church*. Disused T-plan church with regular four-window south front. Sufficient astragals (glazing bars) survive to reveal the delicate narrow horizontal or lying-pane glazing pattern (see also p.7) but there is little trace of interior fittings. *BUILT by Superscription Anno Domini 1842* according to the plaque on the south gable, to serve the scattered population of the area living too far from the nearest churches at Latheron, Watten and Halkirk.

Above *Old Achvanich school.*
Right *Sordale Farm*

Achvanich Farm, Schoolhouse and disused **school** are grouped at the road junction (to Lybster). Nineteenth-century two-storey farmhouse with steading. Plain single-storey school lit by four windows in the long frontage, gazing out over the expanse of moorland; this was frequented by scholars from crofts near and far, a long walk for many of them. Pleasant, white-harled, mid-19th-century, two-storey former schoolhouse.

SORDALE AND STEMSTER

Sordale Farm, mid-19th century
Beautifully constructed group of small-scale farm buildings with two single-storey cottages. It lies opposite Skinnet (see p.102), on the east side of the River Thurso.

Stemster House

45 **Stemster House**, *c*.1870 incorporating earlier house
Tall, white-harled, crowstep-gabled dwelling with generous ashlar margins and dressings. The older house with a projecting stairwell is evident at the rear. An even earlier house was sited in the woods close by, perhaps associated with the roofless, square Stemster **dovecote**, *c*.1700 (see p.103). This cote stands on a rise above Stemster, an early chapel site identified by a plaque inscribed *The Unknown Kirk*.

WATTEN
Watten Cross Roads, on the main Thurso/Wick road, forms the centre of the village with a **tollhouse** of *c*.1815. The parish spans the broad fertile valley stretching from Thurso to Wick, at the foot of wide Loch Watten. Nineteenth-century farming improvements lead to building and rebuilding of farms and their steadings, now with tall 20th-century silos.

Henderson Square, Watten

Henderson Square, 1953-4, James Henderson for Caithness County Council
Sympathetic housing scheme around three sides of a green. The houses vary in style, some gabled and some with deeply recessed arched porches (see p.8). There is pleasing use of local stone, particularly around the porches,

contrasting with the white-harled walls, and the roofs are slated with graded local flagstones. Unfortunately, the scheme is now marred by unsympathetic modern glazing. A **memorial** to Alexander Bain, an inventive pioneer in the application of electricity, stands outside the village hall.

Beaton

Porch, Henderson Square

Church of Scotland (former United Free Church), 1908, D & J R McMillan; simple Gothic with pyramidal-roofed tower.
Achingale Bridge, Watten, 1812-17, Thomas Telford, widened 1933. A handsome, rubble bridge with three segmental arches spanning the Strath Burn, shortly before it becomes the Wick River.

Watten Mains, 1763, white-harled house with central wallhead (nepus) gablet, typical of the better-quality Caithness lairds' houses of the period. Datestone monogrammed for Robert Manson Sinclair of Bridgend and his wife Isabel Sinclair. Later canted dormers. Watten Mains stands close to the burial ground site of the former Watten Parish Church.

Alexander Bain, 1810-77, was born and brought up on a croft at Houstry, near Watten. Bain showed an early interest in clocks and electricity and was apprenticed to a clockmaker in Wick, subsequently moving to Edinburgh and London; he also worked in the USA. During his lifetime he invented the electric clock and electric telegraph, installing the first railway telegraph line between Glasgow and Edinburgh in 1846. He also invented the *electric printing telegraph*, the precursor of the modern fax. Robert P Gunn, *Alexander Bain of Watten: Genius of the North*, 1976

⁴⁶**Achingale Mill**, early 19th century Substantial disused cornmill built into the hillside that carries the mill lade (leet), roofed with local slates. Besides the large overshot waterwheel, there is a small wheel which motivated the automatic stoker feeding chaff to the kiln fire. As the kiln is a later addition to the mill, the automatic feeder and its wheel must also be later modifications. The mill is dated MS 1827 beside the doorway and PS 1885 above; these initials probably refer to the Sandison family of millers. A very fine example of a Caithness cornmill and the use of local building materials.

Historic Scotland

Watten Mains

Beaton

Achingale Mill; note small wheel motivating fuelling of chaff to kiln fire

47 BILBSTER, STIRKOKE AND TANNACH

Bilbster House, from early 18th century
Two-storey, roughly T-plan laird's house settled comfortably amidst trees and garden, unusually sheltered for windswept Caithness, a harmonious blend of local slates and stone. Two storey and attic, originally a five-bay house with a later full-height canted bay right of the main entrance set at right angles to another two-storey crowstepped range. Precise dating is difficult for the site is old and the house may incorporate earlier work.

Stirkoke House, 1858-9 incorporating earlier core, David Bryce
After a fire in 1994, only the shell survives of this baronial mansion with full-height bay windows, angle bartizans and moulded monogrammed doorpiece. Formerly the home of the Horne family.

Top Bilbster House, 18th century with many additions. Above *Stirkoke House*

There are three entries for Bilbster in Timothy Pont's map; *Bylbster, O* (?Old), *Bylbster* and *Nether Bylbster* (see frontispiece and p.4).

48 Haster

A small settlement notable for a terrace of sympathetic local authority bungalows (perhaps W Wilson, former County Architect, c.1970), faced with rich brown local stone and roofed in similar-toned local slates. These later 20th-century homes blend with the traditional built environment of the Caithness countryside.

49 Tannach Mains, late 18th century

Tall, crowstepped farmhouse with flanking wings. Plain but dignified, commanding the undulating farmland and moors west of Wick and Loch Hempriggs and Loch of Yarrows. In sunshine the watery expanses reflect translucent light, illuminating the wide horizons of the agricultural hinterland between the bare moorland of Camster and the populated coastal fringes of Thrumster and Ulbster (see pp.23&24), a typical spectrum of the Caithness landscape.

Sheep shearing at Achorn, Latheron, c.1900

ACKNOWLEDGEMENTS

Without the help, support and hospitality of Geoff and Lyndall Leet, this book could not have been written. George Watson has been unstintingly generous with his vast knowledge of Thurso and Caithness, also with illustrations. Ian Leith, a native Wicker and librarian in Elgin, has advised on Wick and elsewhere: all four have read and commented on various drafts. David Iredale, Archivist, Forres, Moray, translated the brief but complex Latin inscription at Hempriggs, John R Hume permitted me to reproduce his drawing of Canisbay Church, W Ashley Bartlam sketched Castlehill Quarries and Calum McKenzie prepared the maps.

I am grateful to many: Laurie Beaton; John Barnie, Sinclair Macdonald & Son; Joyce Brown, Librarian and the staff at Thurso and Wick Libraries; Dr R G Cant; Lisa Farelly and Trudi Mann, North Highland Archives, Wick; Linda Hardwicke, Almond Design; Helen Leng, Rutland Press; Andrew McLean, Archive Section, Royal Bank of Scotland, Edinburgh; the late Henrietta Munro; Donald Omand, University of Aberdeen; Anne Riches; Harry Gordon Slade; Veronica Steele, National Monuments Record of Scotland, RCAHMS; Robert Steward, Archivist, Inverness; J A Thomson, Planning Officer, Caithness; Margaret Wood, Registrar, Wick; Andrew Wright and Messrs Law & Dunbar-Nasmith, Forres.

For help with illustrations I am indebted to: Miss M Wilkes and staff, Map Library, National Library of Scotland; The Abbot, Nunraw Abbey; Canon Macdonald, St Joachim's, Wick; Dr Joanna Close-Brooks; Dr Neil Jackson; Jo Scott, Dunbeath Preservation Trust; Professor Charles McKean; Dr Deborah Mays and Pam Craig, Historic Scotland; Mike Craig, George Washington Wilson Collection, University of Aberdeen; Ian Sutherland, Wick Society; Les Hester, Forres; C L Dudgeon, Savills, Edinburgh; Clive Richards, North of Scotland Newspapers, Wick; Thurso Museum.

References

The Island of Stroma, Margaret Aitken, c.1972; Caithness: A Cultural Crossroads, (ed.) John R Baldwin, 1982; The Doocots of Caithness, Elizabeth Beaton, 1980; History of Caithness, T Calder, 1887; Exploring Scotland's Heritage: The Highlands, Joanna Close-Brooks, 1986, also revised edn, 1995; A Biographical Dictionary of British Architects 1600-1840, Howard Colvin, 3rd edn, 1995; History of the Episcopal Church in Caithness, J B Craven, 1908; Dictionary of Saints, John J Delaney, 1982; 'The Building of the Roman Catholic Chapel in Wick', 1832-9, Mark Dilworth, Review of Scottish Culture 6, 1990; The British Fisheries Society 1786-1893, Jean Dunlop, 1978; Annals of the Free Church, ii, (ed.) W Ewing, 1914; The Buildings of Scotland: Highlands and Islands, John Gifford, 1992; Old Thurso, Donald Grant, 1965; Alexander Bain of Watten: Genius of the North, Robert P Gunn, Caithness Field Club, 1976; Neil M Gunn: A Highland Life, F R Hart & J B Pick, 1981; Monuments of Industry, G D Hay & G P Stell, 1986; The Architecture of Scottish Post-Reformation Churches 1560-1843, George Hay, 1957; Caithness Family History, John Henderson, 1884; The Industrial Archaeology of Scotland, ii, John Hume, 1977; Fasti of United Free Church of Scotland, (ed.) J A Lamb; The Architectural History of Scotland, 1560-1660, Deborah Howard, 1995; Sir James Gowans, Romantic Rationalist, Duncan McAra, 1975; Telford's Highland Churches, Allan Maclean, 1989; MacFarlane's Geographical Collections, (ed.) A Mitchell & J T Clark, 1906-8; The Castellated and Domestic Architecture of Scotland, David MacGibbon & Thomas Ross, 1887-92; A Wild and Open Sea: The Story of the Pentland Firth, James Miller, 1994; Agricultural Sir John, The Life of Sir John Sinclair of Ulbster, 1754-1835, Rosalind Mitchison, 1962; The Story of the Wick and Ackergill Lifeboats, Jeff Morris, 1984; Scottish Lighthouses, R W Munro, 1979; New Statistical Account, c.1835-45; The Flagstone Industry of Caithness, Donald Omand & John Porter, 1981; The New Caithness Book (ed.) Donald Omand, 1989; Postcards from Caithness, (compiled by) Clive Richards, 1992; Inventory, Caithness, Royal Commission on the Ancient and Historical Monuments of Scotland, 1911; Brochs of Scotland, J N G Ritchie, 1988; The Statistical Account, (ed.) Sir John Sinclair, 1791-9; 'St Peter's Kirk, Thurso, Caithness c.1150-1832', H Gordon Slade & George Watson, Proceedings of the Society of Antiquaries of Scotland, 19, 1989; Robert Dick, Baker of Thurso, Geologist and Botanist, Samuel Smiles, 1878; Statutory List of Buildings of Special Architectural or Historic Interest, Caithness, 1984; The Fortified House in Scotland, v, Nigel Tranter, 1970; Stones: 18th-Century Scottish Gravestones, Betty Willsher & Doreen Hunter, 1978; Stroma, (ed.) Donald Young, 1992. Also John o'Groat Journal, Caithness Courier, Caithness Field Club Bulletin and various local pamphlets.

PICTORIAL GLOSSARY

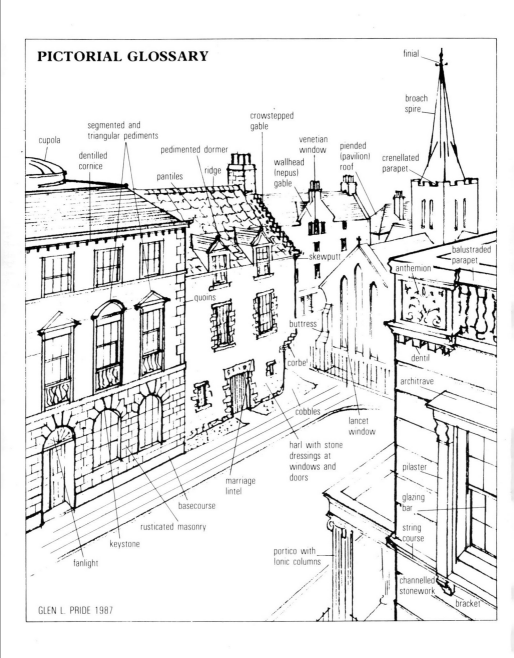

cupola

segmented and triangular pediments

dentilled cornice

pedimented dormer

pantiles

ridge

crowstepped gable

venetian window

wallhead (nepus) gable

piended (pavilion) roof

crenellated parapet

finial

broach spire

skewputt

quoins

buttress

corbel

cobbles

lancet window

harl with stone dressings at windows and doors

marriage lintel

basecourse

rusticated masonry

keystone

fanlight

portico with Ionic columns

balustraded parapet

anthemion

dentil

architrave

pilaster

glazing bar

string course

channelled stonework

bracket

GLEN L. PRIDE 1987

112